U.S. Ballistic Missile Submarines in action

by Al Adcock

Color by Don Greer
Illustrated by Joe Sewell

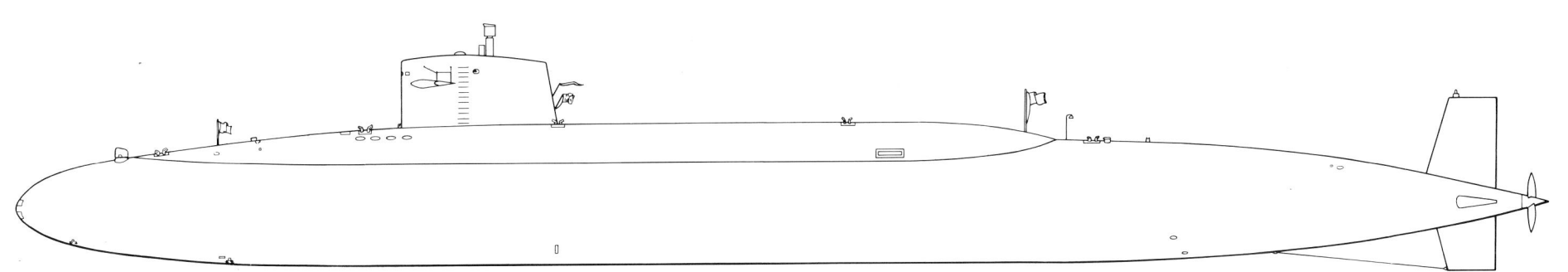

Warships Number 6
squadron/signal publications

The first Trident Fleet Ballistic Missile (FBM) submarine, USS OHIO (SSBN 726), moves at high speed on the surface during her shakedown cruise. She flies her commissioning pennant below the national ensign.

COPYRIGHT © 1993 SQUADRON/SIGNAL PUBLICATIONS, INC.
1115 CROWLEY DRIVE   CARROLLTON, TEXAS 75011-5010
All rights reserved. No part of this publication may be reproduced, stored in a retrieval system or transmitted in any form by any means electrical, mechanical or otherwise, without written permission of the publisher.

ISBN 0-89747-293-4

If you have any photographs of the aircraft, armor, soldiers or ships of any nation, particularly wartime snapshots, why not share them with us and help make Squadron/Signal's books all the more interesting and complete in the future. Any photograph sent to us will be copied and the original returned. The donor will be fully credited for any photos used. Please send them to:

> Squadron/Signal Publications, Inc.
> 1115 Crowley Drive.
> Carrollton, TX 75011-5010.

Acknowledgements

I would like to offer a special thanks to RADM Arlie Campbell for his valued help and encouragement during this project; Thanks Cousin. Further, I would like to thank CDR J.E. Teske, skipper of the USS CASIMIR PULASKI and his crew, Chief of the Boat Zollars of the USS KENTUCKY, and LCDR P. "Trish" McMillan, Bob Steller and Petty Officer Margaret Young of Kings Bay Naval Submarine Base Public Affairs Office for their hospitality during my recent visits. All Americans can rest assured that we have the finest professional military personnel defending us — God speed to you all.

RADM Arlington F. Campbell, USN
U.S. Navy
Strategic Systems Program
Portsmouth Naval Shipyard
General Dynamics
Electric Boat
Graham Gavert
Chief of Naval Information
JOC (SS) Jay M. Davidson, USN

Lockheed
Lee Rowe
Jim Graham
LTV
Debbie Deloach
Albert Adcock IV
National Archives
Navy History Center
Chuck Haberline

Dedication

This book is dedicated to James C. Fahey.

The USS MICHIGAN (SSBN 727), was assigned to Submarine Squadron 17 (SUBRON 17), Naval Submarine Base, Bangor, Washington. Bangor was activated as a Trident submarine base on 1 February 1977 and is located on the Hood Canal, some 155 miles from the Pacific Ocean. (Navy)

INTRODUCTION

The term "Silent Service" evokes images of Second World War submarines complete with foul air, battery acid and diesel fuel. The present day nuclear powered fleet ballistic missile submarine brings a new meaning to the term "Silent Service." With its slippery Black painted stealthy hull and ultra quiet machinery — its silence can be very deadly to any aggressor.

The first submarine was demonstrated in the Thames River, England by its builder, Dutchman Cornelius Drebbel in 1624. The boat was a wooden framework covered with oilsoaked leather and it submerged by contracting the sides thereby reducing internal air volume.

During the revolutionary war an American, David Bushnell, demonstrated the TURTLE, a submersible that featured a hand powered propeller and a ballast tank. The TURTLE made the first combat sortie by a submersible when Bushnell attempted to attack a British warship in New York Harbor; however, he failed in the attempt. Robert Fulton, the inventor of the steam boat, designed a submarine that incorporated the use of compressed air for crew breathing. The design employed a sail for surface propulsion and a hand cranked propeller for propulsion while submerged.

The first successful sinking of a warship by a submarine took place on 17 February 1864, by the Confederate States Ship HUNLEY and this attack revolutionized naval warfare. The CSS HUNLEY attacked and sank the Union Gunboat USS HOUSATONIC in Charleston, SC harbor. The CSS HUNLEY was armed with a torpedo suspended on a long spar ahead of the ship and the attack took place on the surface and at night. Both vessels were lost when the HUNLEY became entangled with the mortally wounded and sinking HOUSATONIC.

The next major development in submarines was undertaken by two Americans, Simon Lake and John P. Holland. Working independently the two designers produced submarines that were accepted by the U.S. Navy, although very reluctantly. Lake's USS SEAL, Holland's (S-1), USS PLUNGER (S-2), and sixteen other boats were all in U.S. Navy service during the early 1900s. The S-1 was purchased by the Navy in April of 1900, launching the submarine service. Holland's company was called the Holland Submarine Torpedo Boat Company with company headquarters at 100 Broadway, New York, NY. The early submarines were called boats because they could be transported by trailer or wagon overland and the name boat just became synonymous with submarines to this day. The largest submarines in the world are still referred to as boats even though they can no longer be transported overland as could the early subs.

In 1900, the Holland Torpedo Boat Company moved to Groton, CT and changed its name to the Electric Boat Company. When contracts from the U.S. Navy were not forthcoming, Simon Lake began selling his submarines to various European countries. Krupp of Germany copied and built upon Lake's designs and by the beginning of World War I had designed a very formidable undersea boat. Holland also sold some boats and designs overseas, mainly to Russia and Great Britain.

It wasn't until 1912 when LT Chester W. Nimitz, who would later become an Admiral and Commander of the U.S. Pacific Fleet during World War II, finally convinced the Navy to install diesel engines in their submarines. The diesel would give more horsepower per fuel consumed, thus giving the submarine a greater range over the conventional gasoline powered types. Diesel fuel also had the advantage of having a much higher flash point than gasoline making it much safer to store aboard the sub.

When the U.S. entered World War I, the sub fleet experienced dismal failures and after the war the Navy sought some answers. In 1919 the Navy was presented with six German U-Boats as war prizes and an immediate analysis of the German subs was undertaken. The Navy team found that the German U-Boats were superior in periscopes, deck guns, diving ability and diesel/electric propulsion. As a result of their findings, the team recommended that the Navy Bureau of Ships (BUSHIPS) consider a design that incorporated all of the features of the German boats.

BUSHIPS came out with a design called the V-Class that employed most of the German improvements. In all, nine boats were built in five different classes. Seven were built by the Portsmouth Naval Shipyard and one each were built by Mare Island Shipyard and the Electric Boat Company. All of the nine boats served during World War II and all but the USS ARGOUNAT (SM-1/SS-166) survived. The last two V-Class boats, USS CACHALOT (SS-170) and USS CUTTLEFISH (SS-171), were the first U.S. built submarines to employ an all welded hull.

The years between wars saw submarine designers on both sides of the oceans striving to improve on existing designs. When the Second World War began, the German Kriegsmarine was equipped with the Type VII and IX U-Boats which had been derived from their earlier U-81 series first introduced during 1916. The U.S. Navy had the ALBACORE, GAR and TROUT Class fleet submarines, all displacing 1,525 tons and based on earlier U.S. and German designs. The Japanese Imperial Navy relied upon earlier designs that were influenced by American, German and French submarines. The Japanese employed a variety of different sizes of subs during the war, ranging from their midget two man submarine (used to attack Pearl Harbor) to the gigantic 394 foot long and 3,530 ton displacement I-400 class. With the exception of a few oddities, the Japanese used conventionally designed and operated submarines for coastal patrol and long range duties.

The Soviet Union relied upon a few subs purchased from foreign ship builders, such

The USS NAUTILUS (SSN 571) was the world's first nuclear powered ship. The NAUTILUS was launched on 21 January 1954 and commissioned on 30 September 1954. Built by Electric Boat at Groton, CT the ship is now on permanent display at the Nautilus Memorial and Submarine Force Library and Museum, Groton, CT. (Electric Boat)

as Electric Boat Company and Vickers of Great Britain, as well as their own ship builders in Leningrad, Gorki and Siberia. Great Britain entered World War II with the fewest submarines of any major power and twenty percent of those were very old and not suitable for war service. Regardless, they were placed in harms way. The French submarine fleet in many ways resembled that of the British in that they had many old subs with a few new designs being built when they were overrun by the Germans in June of 1940.

Propulsion Development

During the early days of World War II, the Germans took the lead in the development of new propulsion systems to replace the diesel/electric drive. Professor/Doctor Hellmuth Walter of the Walter Design Bureau had proposed to the German Navy the use of a diesel/turbine engine power plant to be installed in a small U-boat. This project became known as Project V and was one of many unconventional ways to manufacture and propel submarines tested by the Germans during the war. The Walter engine, as it became known, was to be fuelled with hydrogen peroxide (HTP) in high test form, called perhydrol. The advantage of HTP fuel was its ability to break down into water and oxygen which would provide a submerged U-boat with air to run its diesel without resorting to the *schnorkel*.

ADM Hyman G. Rickover was given credit as being the father of the United States Nuclear Navy. ADM Rickover was born in Russia in 1900 and emigrated with his parents to the U.S. when he was six years old. In 1948 he was placed in charge of the Naval Reactors Branch, a post he held until 1982. (Navy.)

The *schnorkel* was devised by the Dutch before World War II and was made available to German scientists in May 1940 when Holland and the low countries were overrun. It wasn't until 1943 that a *schnorkel* equipped U-boat became operational in the battle for the Atlantic. The disadvantages of the HTP fuel became apparent once the Walter engine was put to the test. The Walter engine burned up to 30 times as much HTP as conventional diesel fuel. The Germans actually built seven such systems and installed them in seven U-boats of the Type XVIIA and Type XVIIB. All seven were scuttled at the end of the Second World War II, but two were recovered and raised. One went to Great Britain (U-1407) and one to the Unites States (U-1406). The British experimented with the Walter engine system and then built two submarines to explore the possibility of using the closed Walter system of propulsion. The two subs built by the Royal Navy were the HMS EXPLORER and the HMS EXCALIBUR, and both were purely experimental in nature and did not have torpedo tubes. The HTP fuel was in many ways as dangerous as gasoline and many accidents and fires were reported, so many that EXPLORER was referred to as the EXPLODER. The Walter system, although never successful in submarines, found its way into torpedoes. The new advanced lightweight torpedoes being deployed by the USN and Royal Navy employ at Walter closed type system of propulsion.

Following World War II, the U.S. Navy saw no advantage to powering their subs with the Walter system as they were working on a power plant that would revolutionized submarine propulsion — nuclear power.

The Westinghouse Electric Company was authorized by the newly formed Atomic Energy Commission to go ahead with the design, construction and operation of a prototype nuclear propulsion power plant during 1948. The Bettis Atomic Power Laboratories, Pittsburgh, Pennsylvania, operated by Westinghouse, was charged with putting nuclear theory into practical use.

In August of 1950, President Harry S. Truman signed Public Law 674 which authorized the construction of the USS NAUTILUS, a submarine that was to be fitted with the first nuclear reactor power plant. During 1951 BUSHIPS awarded a contract to the Electric Boat Company for construction of the hull, while Westinghouse was awarded the contract for the nuclear reactor. CAPT (later Admiral) Hyman G. Rickover was appointed to oversee this historic program. The USS NAUTILUS (SSN-571) was commissioned on 30 September 1954 and on 17 January 1955, CAPT Eugene P. Wilkinson was able to signal "Underway on nuclear power."

The power plant in the NAUTILUS was a Westinghouse S2W reactor which used the pressurized water concept. Water heated by the reactor was used to produce steam which turned the turbine reduction gear and then was condensed back into water and recycled. The reactor core is cooled by the secondary water system and also turned into steam. The steam produced by the reactor was also used to drive the sub's turbo-generators for electric power. This pressurized water type of power plant became the standard for nuclear powered ships and submarines in the U.S. Navy.

There was one other type of nuclear power plant designed and built by the General Electric Company and it utilized the liquid metal (sodium) concept for cooling. The S2G liquid sodium-cooled reactor gave a much more efficient transfer of heat, but technical and safety considerations outweighed its mechanical advantages. The sodium-cooled reactor (S2G) was installed in the USS SEAWOLF (SSN 575) and she was commissioned on 30 March 1957. After some two years of operation, in which SEAWOLF had sailed over 71,000 miles, the liquid sodium-cooled reactor was replaced by the more conventional pressurized water type. The former Soviet Union though still employs liquid metal reactors in their MIKE, ALFA and SIERRA class submarines.

Early Missile Experiments

During 1942, two Germans, Doctor Ernest Steinhoff, a Peenemunde rocket scientist working for Werner Von Braun, and his brother CAPT Fritz Steinhoff, of the U-551 contrived a plan to install rockets on a U-Boat. A Type VIIC U-Boat was fitted with a rack that could hold six 300MM *Wurfkoper 42 Spreng* tactical rockets. The tests were successful and a launch was made from a depth of twelve meters. The test results were shown to ADM Karl Donitz and his staff, but the idea was turned down as impractical and of no value to the German war effort. Additionally, it was felt that it would tie up a fleet of U-boats that could be used to sink allied convoys.

During 1943, a plan was devised to place German A-4 (V-2) rockets in floating containers and then tow them by U-Boat to the United States. Once offshore, their ballast tanks would be filled with water, righting the container. Then the missiles would be fired at major cities on the U.S. East Coast. Contracts were actually let to the Stettin Shipyard in Poland for three such containers for test purposes, but by the time the war ended none had been produced.

Following the end of World War II, many German scientists fell into the hands of the Americans and Soviets and a number of them were brought to the United States and the Soviet Union. The Soviets experimented with the containerized rocket idea, while early U.S. tests focused on the German FZG-76 (V-1) Buzz Bomb. Called the Loon in Navy service, the captured Buzz Bombs were as dangerous to the sub's crew as to the enemy and many missiles exploded during launch. In 1947, the Navy began to experiment with the launching of the Loon and later Regulus I and Regulus II missiles from the decks of surfaced submarines.

The first firing of a missile from the deck of a U.S. Navy submarine occurred in July of 1947 when a Loon was launched from the deck of the USS CUSK (SS-348). Two other submarines were also fitted with launching gear to fire the Loon, the USS BARBERO (SS-317) and USS CARBONERO (SS-337). The CUSK became the first Navy sub to be designated as a SSG, the G standing for guided missile. The Loon program led to the development of the turbojet powered SSM-N-8 Regulus I. The LTV-built Regulus I had a top speed of 600 mph and it could be armed with a nuclear warhead. The USS TUNNY (SS 282) was modified to carry and test the new Regulus I and three submarines were built for the express purpose of launching the missiles. The USS GRAYBACK (SSG-574) and USS GROWLER (SSG-577), both diesel powered submarines, and the USS HALIBUT (SSG/N-597), a nuclear powered submarine. The missiles were carried in a dry deck hangar that could hold up to five missiles. A further development of the Regulus carrying submarines was the USS PERMIT which was to be assigned the hull number (SSGN-593). In the event, the PERMIT project never got past the model stage, but it was to feature four dry deck hangars, two forward on the bow and two on either side of the sail.

An LTV N2 Loon guided missile is positioned on the catapult launch rails of the USS CARBONERO (SS 337) on 26 August 1949. The missile was overall Natural Metal and it carried the number 824 on the nose in Red with Red and White stripes on the fuselage and rudder. (National Archives)

The USS CUSK (SS 348) was first U.S. Navy submarine to fire a guided missile from her deck. These early LTV-2 Loon missiles often exploded on launch, like this one did during April of 1947. The LTV-2 Loon was a copy of the German V-1 Buzz Bomb. (National Archives)

A water proof deck shelter was added to the USS BARBERO (SS 317) during 1958 so she could carry the Regulus I missile while submerged. To fire the missile, the submarine surfaced and the Regulus was removed from the shelter and fitted to the launch rails. (National Archives)

The Regulus I entered service with both the surface and submarine fleet during 1955. A later development of the Regulus I, the Regulus II (SSM-N-9), also produced by LTV, was the only Supersonic Cruise Missile ever deployed by the U.S. Navy. The GROWLER, GRAYBACK and HALIBUT were to deploy with the Regulus II, but with the development of the Polaris ballistic missile, the Regulus II program was cancelled during 1958.

The GRAYBACK was later converted to the LPSS (Landing Personnel Submarine) role and used to deliver U.S. Navy SEAL Teams and Marine Long Range Recon Patrols (LRRPs) onto hostile beaches. The missile compartments were used to house Swimmer Delivery Vehicles (SDVs). The conversion of the GROWLER was cancelled due to the high cost of the GRAYBACK's conversion. The HALIBUT was later used to test the fifty foot Deep Submergence Rescue Vehicle (DSRV).

The USS GRAYBACK (SSG 574) was the first U.S. submarine built to carry and launch guided missiles. A Regulus II missile has been rolled out of the bow hangar and preparations are underway to test fire the missile. The GRAYBACK was fitted with two hangars that could accommodate four Regulus II missiles. (LTV)

The USS HALIBUT (SSGN 587) launches a Regulus I guided missile on 31 March 1960. With this launch the HALIBUT became the first U. S. nuclear-powered submarine to launch a cruise missile. The HALIBUT became obsolete when the Polaris submarine GEORGE WASHINGTON became operational during November 1960. (National Archives)

USS GROWLER (SSG 577) was a sister ship to the GRAYBACK and was also fitted with bow mounted hangars. These hangars were eleven feet high and seventy feet long and could accommodate up to five Regulus I missiles. The missile launcher was located between the hangar doors and the sail. (Portsmouth Naval Shipyard)

Ballistic Missile Development

On 8 November 1955, the U.S. Secretary of Defense Charles Wilson gave the go ahead for the U.S. Army and Navy to proceed jointly with the development of the IRBM #2 (Intermediate Range Ballistic Missile Number Two). The Jupiter program, as it became known, began the development of both liquid and solid propellant missiles to be used both from ships and land bases. The Navy proceeded with the solid propellant version after determining that liquid propellants were inherently dangerous and not suitable for use aboard submarines.

The Soviet Union's Submarine Launched Ballistic Missile (SLBM) program continued development of the German A-4 (V-2) liquid fueled rocket and installed them in the GOLF, HOTEL, YANKEE and DELTA classes of Ballistic Missile Submarines. The Soviet's experienced at least three submarine losses due to problems with the liquid fueled rockets.

On 8 December 1956, the U.S. Navy was given the authorization to proceed on their own with the development of the solid propellant Polaris A-1 Submarine Launched Ballistic Missile (SLBM) and on 18 December 1956, the joint Army/Navy Ballistic Missile Committee was dissolved (the Army opted to continue development of liquid fueled missiles). The Polaris, named for the North Star, was a two stage, 28,000 pound missile with a range of 1,380 miles. Guidance was an inertial system that relied completely on internal control. The Polaris (UGM-27) was fitted with a single W-47 thermonuclear warhead with a yield of 500 kilotons (KT).

Development, production and testing was undertaken by Lockheed and Aerojet. Lockheed built the missile airframe and Aerojet built the rocket motor. The guidance system was developed by MIT and manufactured by General Electric and Hughes. The first few flight tests of the Polaris A-1 did not go well and it wasn't until 20 April 1959, during the fifth flight, that a successful launch/flight occurred. Testing proceeded with the installation of the guidance equipment and thermonuclear warhead during 1959 and 1960. Events started moving rapidly toward the day when the newly built USS GEORGE WASHINGTON (SSBN 598) would be mated with the Polaris. On 14 April 1960, the Polaris A-1 was successfully launched from underwater during a test at San Clemente Island, California. Just three months later, the first U.S. Ballistic Missile submarine, USS GEORGE WASHINGTON, launched a Polaris A-1 while submerged. Seven months later, on 15 November 1960, the GEORGE WASHINGTON deployed with a full load of sixteen Polaris A-1 missiles; the first Fleet Ballistic Missile (FBM) submarine deterrent patrol.

The Polaris A-1 was deployed with the GEORGE WASHINGTON and ETHAN ALLEN Class submarines and was in service for five years until it was replaced by the improved Polaris A-2. The A-2 had a range of 1,800 miles, a 400 mile improvement over the A-1. The A-2 stayed in service until September of 1964 when the much improved A-3 replaced it. The Polaris A-3 offered a range of over 2,800 miles and the redesigned nose cone contained three W-58, 200 KT thermonuclear warheads mounted in MK-2 re-entry vehicles. The A-3 became operational on 28 September 1964 when the USS DANIEL WEBSTER (SSBN-626) began her initial deterrent patrol with a full load of sixteen SLBMs. The Polaris A-3 stayed in service until October of 1981 when it was replaced by the Poseidon C-3.

The U.S. produced a total of 1,153, A-1, A-2, and A-3s and deployed a total of 916 of all types. Some of those not expended in tests or deployed were sold to the United Kingdom to be deployed in their RESOLUTION Class FBM submarines. The Polaris was carried by all classes of U.S. FBM submarines except the OHIO Class. The GEORGE WASHINGTON Class carried the A-1 and A-3. The ETHAN ALLEN Class was fitted with the A-2 and during their second overhaul backfitted with the A-3. The LAFAYETTE Class, like the ETHAN ALLEN Class, was initially fitted with A-2, with the A-3 being backfitted during overhaul periods. The JAMES MADISON Class was originally fitted with the Polaris A-2 but the Poseidon C-3 was backfitted during their first overhaul period. The BENJAMIN FRANKLIN Class was also originally A-3 equipped but received the improved Poseidon during their first overhaul.

In 1962, President John F. Kennedy authorized the sale of Polaris A-3 missiles (less warheads) to the United Kingdom. The missiles and subsystems, such as launch controls, were installed in HMS RESOLUTION, HMS RENOWN, HMS REPULSE and HMS REVENGE. HMS RESOLUTION made her first deterrent patrol out of Faslane, Scotland during June of 1968. The British, like the U.S. Navy, operate their subs with two separate crews. While one is at sea, the other crew is training or on leave. The British call their crews Port and Starboard, while the U.S. crews are called Blue and Gold. All of the Royal Navy FBM subs are based with Number 10 Squadron at Faslane Royal Navy Facility in Scotland near Holy Loch where the first U.S. Polaris boats were based.

Continued development of the Polaris A-3 led to the development of the Polaris B-3 during 1963 (which would later become the Poseidon C-3, UGM-73A). The Poseidon was a much larger diameter missile, seventy-four inches compared to fifty-four inches for the Polaris. The length of the Poseidon was increased to thirty-four feet, some two feet longer than the earlier Polaris. The biggest increase was in the missile's weight. The

Submarine Launched Ballistic Missiles

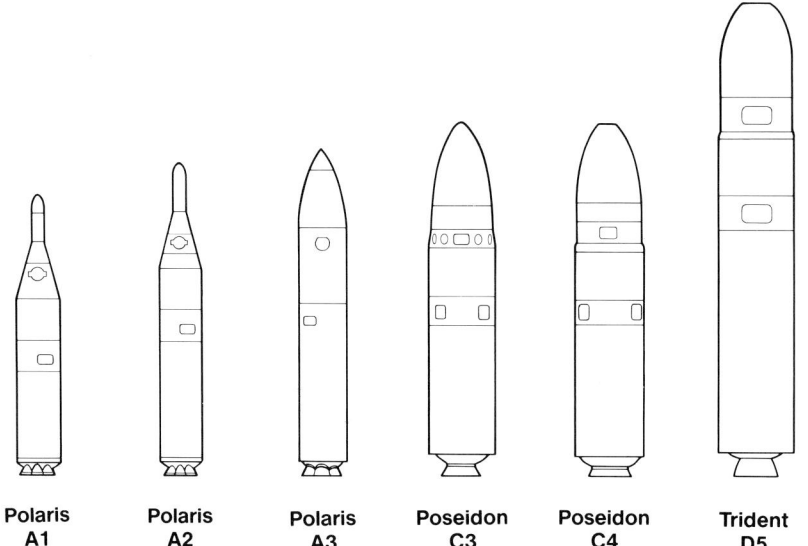

Polaris A1   Polaris A2   Polaris A3   Poseidon C3   Poseidon C4   Trident D5

Poseidon C-3 weighed 65,000 pounds, while the Polaris A-3 weighed only 35,700 pounds. The range for both missiles remained 2,800 miles. The reason for the dramatic increase in weight was the increased weight of the warheads and their associated re-entry vehicles. The C-3 could carry up to ten 50 KT, W-68 thermonuclear warheads mounted in Mark 3 re-entry vehicles. The warheads, called MIRVs (Multiple Independently Targetable Re-entry Vehicles) were independently targeted against ten different targets. The Poseidon was backfitted to the LAFAYETTE Class during their second overhaul periods (beginning in June of 1975) which included removing the missile tube inner liners to increase the tube diameter. The C-3 was backfitted to the JAMES MADISON Class during their first overhaul period (March 1971) and the BENJAMIN FRANKLIN Class was also backfitted with the C-3 during their first overhaul period (November of 1972).

The Poseidon C-3 became operational on 31 March 1971 aboard the USS JAMES MADISON and remained in service until President George Bush began his nuclear reduction initiate during 1991. As the Poseidon became operational, tests were underway to reach a potential range of 4,000 miles. A total of 619 Poseidon C-3s were produced by Lockheed at Sunnyvale, California. At one time during the 1970s, a total of 496 were deployed aboard thirty-one FBMs in three different classes. The Poseidon long range tests eventually led to the development of the Trident I C-4.

The Trident I program came about mainly from the desire to develop an SLBM with a much greater range than the Poseidon. This greater range would allow the subs to operate much farther from their intended targets, making it much more difficult for them to be detected by hostile anti-submarine land and sea based forces. One other reason for the development of the Trident I was to counter development and deployment of improved land and sea based missiles by the Soviet Union. The U.S. was striving to reach nuclear missile parity with the Soviet Union, something that they never numerically achieved, while technological superiority was another matter.

The Trident I (UGM-96A) is a three stage, solid fuel, stellar and intertially guided missile that weigh 73,000 pounds when armed with eight 100 KT W-76 warheads. The Trident I was capable of carrying up to fourteen warheads, but the range is greatly reduced due to the increased weight of the additional warheads. The Trident I C-4 and the Poseidon C-3 are both thirty-four feet long and both have a diameter of seventy-four inches. The similar dimensions allowed the Trident to be backfitted into the submarines that had been modified to carry the Poseidon, but only six of the BENJAMIN FRANKLIN and six JAMES MADISON CLASS SSBNS were fitted with the improved Trident I, as were the first eight OHIO Class SSBNs (726-733)

The Trident I finally gave the U.S. Navy the range it was looking for, 4,600 miles, which enabled the sub to operate in a much broader expanse of ocean, making it much more difficult to detect by hostile forces. The increase in range came about by utilizing three stages and a unique aerospike, an extendable nose faring that performed the function of making the missile more aerodynamic. The aerospike is extended once the missile is in the air and remains retracted while the missile is in the missile tube to keep its length compatible with the submarines missile tube.

The USS FRANCIS SCOTT KEY (SSBN-657) was the first of the non-OHIO Class subs to be backfitted with the Trident I C-4 and she made her first C-4 deterrent patrol on 20 October 1979, from Charleston, S.C. The first purpose built Trident FBM, the USS OHIO (SSBN-726) deployed from Bangor Naval Submarine Base, Washington on 6 September 1982 with CAPT Alton K. Thompson in command of the Blue crew.

In October of 1980, the Secretary of Defense, Harold Brown, gave the go ahead on the development of the Trident II D-5. The D-5, designated the UGM-133, would give the submarines the ability to target the Soviet Union from almost anywhere in the world where there was water to float the submarines. The D-5 would take advantage of the enlarged missile tubes of the OHIO Class.

A Polaris A2 Submarine Launched Ballistic Missile (SLBM) breakes the surface and lifts off down range during a successful test firing. The A-2 had a range of 1,700 miles. (Navy)

Riding on a piller of fire, a Polaris A-3 SLBM begins it flight down range during a test launch from a submerged FBM submarine. The A-3 had increased range and an improved guidance system. (Navy)

The Trident II D-5 has a length of forty-five feet and a diameter of eighty-three inches. The weight is increased, due to the enlarged first stage, to 130,000 pounds, a considerable increase over the 73,000 pound Trident I C-4. Range of the Trident II D-5 is listed as the same as the C-4, but in reality it is probably closer to 8,000 miles but with a greatly reduced payload of warheads. The lengthened first stage and enlarged second stage are designed to increase range and to get the missile into outer space where the stellar navigation equipment can guide the multiple re-entry vehicles to their targets. The D-5 is capable of carrying anywhere from eight to fourteen W-87 thermonuclear 300 KT weapons. Lockheed Missile and Space Co. built all of the D-5 missiles, as well as all of the previous Polaris and Poseidon missiles.

The USS TENNESSEE (SSBN 734) was the first of the OHIO Class to be fitted with the Trident II and she became operational, during 1988, from Kings Bay Naval Submarine Base, Georgia. The eight earlier OHIO class are to be backfitted with the Trident II to replace their Trident I; however, due to the continuing improvement of relations with the Commonwealth of Independent States (CIS) this backfitting might be put on hold. It is anticipated that by the year 2010, only the Trident II will be serving on the OHIO Class FBMs.

The British are also buying the new Trident II D-5 and they will install them in their new VANGUARD Class FBM. Once the class is commissioned the submarines will sail to Kings Bay Naval Submarine Base, Georgia to be fitted with the their Trident II D-5 missiles. The VANGUARD Class consists of four FBM submarines that are being built by Vickers Shipbuilding and all should be operational by 1995. Once the missiles are installed at Kings Bay, the Royal Navy submarines will return to their home base at Faslane, Scotland. The Vanguard Class carry only sixteen Trident II missiles as compared to twenty-four in the OHIO class.

Ballistic missile launching from a submarine, once all command and control procedures have been carried out by the captain and launch control team, is accomplished by a steam generation system. Super heated gas is exhausted through water at the base of the launch tube to create steam. The steam build up drives the missile out of the tube and clear of the surface of the water where the missile's first stage rocket motor is ignited. All FBM submarines presently in service employ this type of missile launch system. The earlier GEORGE WASHINGTON and ETHAN ALLEN Classes first employed a compressed air type of launch system, but with the increase in the size and weight of the newer missiles, an improved type of system became necessary to get the missile out of the tube and into the air for first stage ignition.

When the Poseidon or Trident missiles are not aboard the FBM submarines they are stored at a Strategic Weapons Facility (SWF), either at Bangor, Washington or Kings Bay, Georgia (for Tridents) and Charleston, S.C. for the Poseidons. The storage facility provides maintenance, construction upgrading and refitting. Security at the SWF is provided by the U.S. Marine Corps. The Marines stationed at the SWF are a highly motivated group consisting of three platoons whose mission is to protect the missiles and nuclear arsenal.

Pre-Trident FBM submarines are supported at fleet level by submarine tenders. In late 1981 there were five sub tenders dedicated to the servicing of FBM submarines. One ship, the USS PROTEUS (AS-19) was due to be decommissioned and retired during early 1992. The four remaining tenders are the USS HUNLEY (AS-31) and USS HOLLAND (AS-32), although the HUNLEY Class ships are both now configured for servicing attack subs. The remaining two are the SIMON LAKE Class: USS SIMON LAKE (AS-33) and USS CANOPUS (AS-34). The CANOPUS is home ported at Kings Bay and the SIMON LAKE recently departed to become the last tender to serve at Holy Loch,

The Poseidon C3 missile was larger, heavier, had a longer range and carried more warheads than the earlier Polaris missiles.

The first Trident II D-5 performance evaluation missile (PEM-1) was launched from the USS TENNESSEE on 21 March 1989 off the coast of Cape Canaveral, Florida. (Lockheed)

Scotland. The tenders provide crew quarters and office spaces when the subs are exchanging crews. They also provide missile loading facilities to all classes of FBMs except the OHIO Class. The tenders are self-sufficient and have the capability to deploy to other ports in the event of a national emergency or for security, and the ability to work out of a civilian port in reaction to wartime conditions.

The tenders conduct all forms of heavy maintenance on the submarines and have the cranes used to load and unload the Poseidon missiles. The Trident missile, however, is too long and must be handled in an explosive handing wharf that is covered to prevent spy satellites from viewing the missile handling procedures. One end is left open so that only the stern of the submarine can be seen from the air.

The ROBERT E. LEE (SSBN 601) offloads Polaris A-3 missiles at the Strategic Weapons Facility Explosive Handing Wharf, Bangor, Washington on 25 February 1982. A security force Marine observes the removal of one of the missiles from a port missile tube. (Lockheed)

The Explosive Handling Wharf (EHW), Naval Submarine Base Kings Bay, Georgia. The EHW is used to load Trident missiles hidden from spy satellites. The south end is left open to comply with the provisions of the Salt Treaty and the six towers act as lightning arrestors. (Navy via Bob Steller)

The USS CANOPUS (AS 34) with four FBM submarines moored alongside for refitting at Kings Bay, Georgia during 1991. The deck of the starboard sub closest to the CANOPUS is stacked with supplies, such as food and paper goods, that will be used on her upcoming patrol (that could last up to 90 days at sea). (Navy)

GEORGE WASHINGTON Class

The GEORGE WASHINGTON Class of nuclear submarines were the first Fleet Ballistic Missile (FBM) submarines to enter service. The USS GEORGE WASHINGTON (SSBN 598) was originally laid down as the attack submarine USS SCORPION (SSN 589) and construction of the attack boat was well underway when the progress of the cooperative Army/Navy Jupiter program led to a decision to proceed with the development of the Polaris missile and a companion FBM submarine to carry the weapon system. BUSHIPS decided that SCORPION was to be converted to the first FBM sub.

In January of 1958, construction of the first three FBM subs began and the SS-589 was officially renamed GEORGE WASHINGTON and redesignated SSGN-598. In June of 1958, the first three FBMs had their designations changed to SSBN to signify their ballistic missile role. The former SCORPION's hull was cut in half just behind the sail and a 130 foot missile section was inserted. The missile section housed sixteen Polaris A-1 ballistic missiles each with a range of 1,200 miles.

Electric Boat was contracted to build the first two FBMs, USS GEORGE WASHINGTON (SSBN 598) and USS PATRICK HENRY (SSBN 599). The GEORGE WASHINGTON was launched on 9 June 1959 and commissioned on the 30 December of that same year. The third ship in the class, USS THEODORE ROOSEVELT (SSBN 600), was built by the Mare Island Shipyard in Vallejo, California and was commissioned on 13 February 1961. The fourth GEORGE WASHINGTON Class was the USS ROBERT E. LEE (SSBN 601) and she was built by the Newport News Shipbuilding and Drydock Company at Newport News, Virginia. The USS ROBERT E. LEE was commissioned on 18 December 1959. The fifth ship in the class was the USS ABRAHAM LINCOLN (SSBN 602) and she was built by Portsmouth Naval Shipyard in Kittery, Maine and commissioned on 11 March 1961.

After the usual sea trials and fitting out, the USS GEORGE WASHINGTON made its first deterrent patrol, loaded with sixteen Polaris A-1 (UGM-27A) ballistic missiles, from Charleston Harbor on 15 November 1960. Following close behind was the USS PATRICK HENRY, which sailed out of Charleston on 30 December 1960 on her first deterrent patrol. The GEORGE WASHINGTON returned to New London, CT after being on patrol for sixty-seven days, sixty-six days and ten hours of that having been spent submerged.

GEORGE WASHINGTON Class subs were all 382 feet long and 33 feet at the beam. Displacement on the surface was some 5,900 tons and submerged displacement was 6,900 tons. They were all powered by a S5W Westinghouse pressurized water cooled reactor that provided steam to the two General Electric geared turbines that drove a single seven blade screw. The reactor produced 15,000 equivalent horse power giving the ship a rated top speed of fifteen plus knots on the surface and twenty plus knots submerged. Maximum diving depth was more than 900 feet.

GEORGE WASHINGTON Class subs were built using the BUSHIPS design number SCB-180A. Owing to its original fast attack boat design, the class was armed with six torpedo tubes in the bow. These 21 inch tubes carried the Mark 16 Mod 6 or Mk 37 torpedoes until 1974 when these were replaced by the Gould Mark 48 torpedo. The Mk 48 is a 3,500 pound dual purpose torpedo which could attack surface or submerged targets and can be either free running or wire guided. The Mk 48 was powered by a liquid propellant called Otto fuel and had a range of over twenty-three miles and a top speed of over fifty miles per hour.

In the event of a nuclear reactor shutdown while at sea, all GEORGE WASHINGTON Class (in fact all USN nuclear submarines) are equipped with an auxiliary stand by diesel/electric drive for emergency power and propulsion. The diesel (or outboard motor) received air through the snorkel; however, if near the surface, and operating the diesel was would not be desirable because of hostile forces in the area, the electric

FBM Development

USS Scorpion

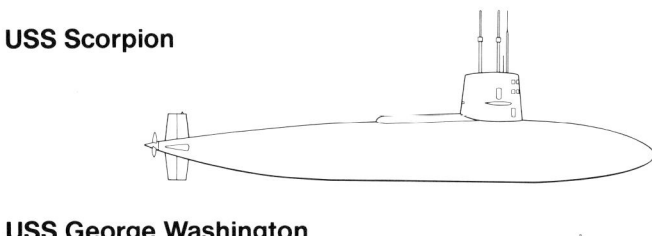

USS George Washington

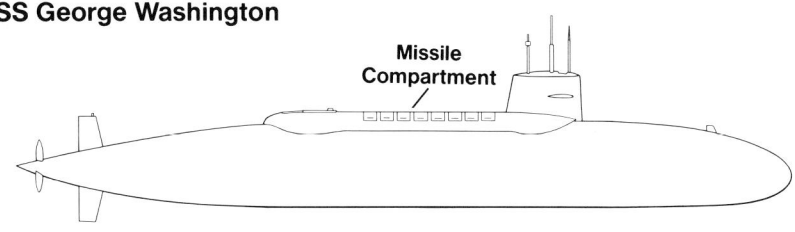

The USS GEORGE WASHINGTON (SSBN 598) was originally laid down as USS SCORPION (SSN 589), but with the success of the Polaris Project, the SCORPION was cut in half and a 130 foot missile compartment, complete with sixteen missile tubes, was inserted. Re-named the USS GEORGE WASHINGTON was built by Electric Boat, Groton, CT and launched on 9 June 1959. (Navy)

motor could be engaged. Speed and endurance were greatly reduced, however, because of the limited battery power available.

All of the GEORGE WASHINGTON Class were manned by twelve officers and a complement of 127 enlisted men. This comprised a full crew. The ships could be operated with less crew, but with a much greater work load and responsibility on all personnel. The class operated for four years until it was time for the first overhaul and refit period in 1964.

During 1964, the GEORGE WASHINGTON became the first of the class to enter the overhaul facility at Electric Boat. The overhaul consisted of refueling the reactor and backfitting of the Polaris A-3 (UGM-27C) weapons system to replace the Polaris A-1. The A-3 offered some improvement in range and guidance systems. With the backfitting of the A-3 came a change in the missile launch system. The compressed air launch system was replaced by the gas generation/steam method. The air launch system could not build up enough pressure fast enough to eject the heavier A-3 missile from the tube. By 1967, all GEORGE WASHINGTON Class FBMs had been backfitted to the A-3.

During the middle 1970s the Class was again upgraded with the improved Polaris A-3T. The A-3T offered an improved range of over 3,000 miles and carried higher yield thermonuclear weapons with increased accuracy of the MIRVed warheads.

During 1981, the USS THEODORE ROOSEVELT and USS ABRAHAM LINCOLN had their missiles offloaded at Charleston, SC and were decommissioned and deactivated at Bremerton, Washington. The missile compartment was removed and cut up and then they were stripped of all nuclear and other sensitive equipment and finally broken up and disposed of as scrap.

The USS PROTEUS (AS 19) loads a Polaris A-1 missile aboard USS GEORGE WASHINGTON in the Holy Loch, Scotland in early 1962. The PROTEUS was the first sub tender (AS) converted for servicing the Fleet Ballistic Missile (FBM) submarines. The PROTEUS was withdrawn from FBM service during 1991. (National Archives)

The three remaining ships of the class, GEORGE WASHINGTON, ROBERT E. LEE and PATRICK HENRY, were used as attack submarines (SSNs) for a short while following the removal of all related Polaris equipment during 1981. The ROBERT E. LEE and PATRICK HENRY, after their missile compartment and reactors were removed, were also disposed of as scrap during 1983. The subs were decommissioned for two reasons: first to comply with the Salt I Treaty and secondly because they had basically reached the end of their useful life span, having been in service for over twenty years and having been subjected to the rigors of the constant exposure to salt water and high hull pressure cycles on their hulls.

The names of THEODORE ROOSEVELT, ABRAHAM LINCOLN and GEORGE WASHINGTON would later be assigned to the NIMITZ Class of nuclear aircraft carriers designated as CVN 71 thru 73 respectively.

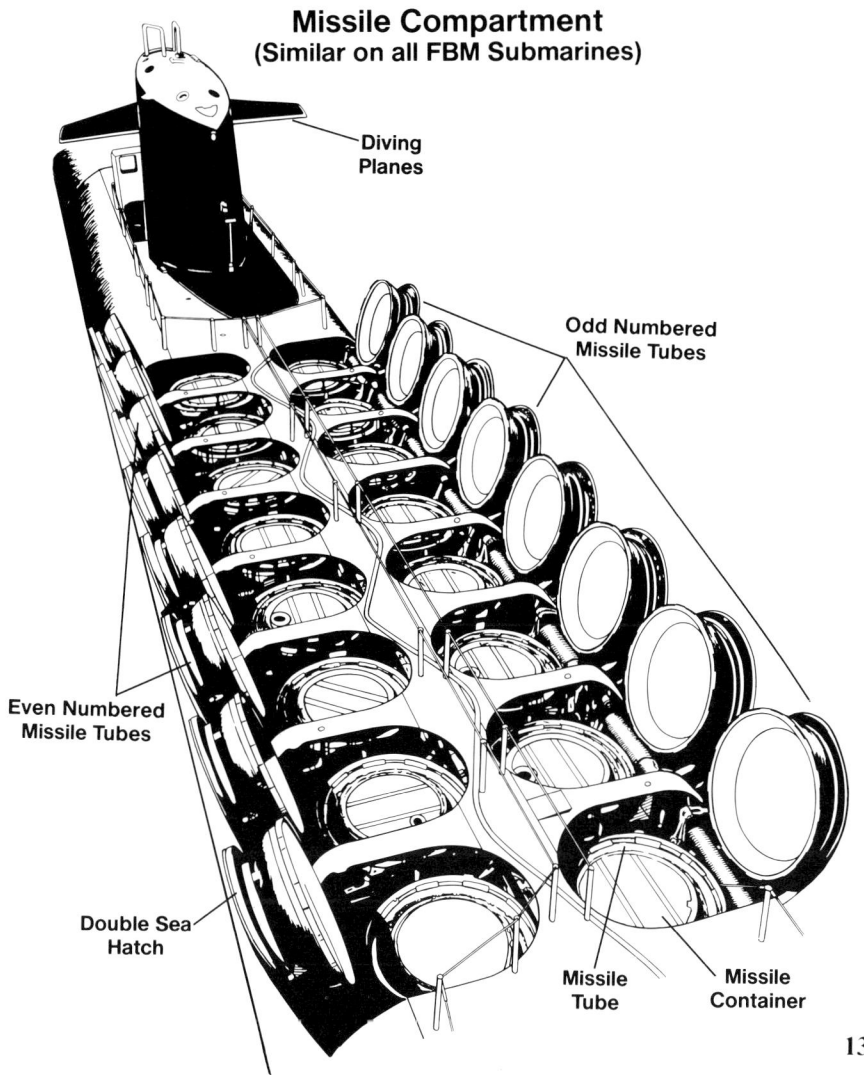

Missile Compartment
(Similar on all FBM Submarines)

A sailor paints out the sail number (598) on the USS GEORGE WASHINGTON during 1960 prior to her going on her first patrol in the Atlantic. U.S. submarines were originally painted in a Black and Gray scheme, but that was soon changed to a Black (above the water line) scheme. (National Archives)

President Dwight D. Eisenhower at the controls of USS PATRICK HENRY (SSBN 599), the second fleet ballistic missile submarine to be launched. President Eisenhower had signed the appropriation bills authorizing the construction of the five GEORGE WASHINGTON class during 1958. (Navy via Lockheed)

The USS PATRICK HENRY (SSBN 599) underway out of Apra Harbor, Guam on 20 December 1978. The PATRICK HENRY had made her first operational patrol on 30 December 1960 out of Charleston Harbor. On 24 October 1981, the PATRICK HENRY was reclassified as an SSN and used for anti-submarine training (ASW) until decommissioned on 25 May 1984. (Navy)

ADM Hyman G. Rickover is welcomed aboard USS PATRICK HENRY for sea trials in March of 1960. ADM Rickover personally selected every officer in the FBM program and sailed on every sea trial involving a nuclear submarine until he was 81 years old. (National Archives)

Two machinist mates discuss the operations of the number 3 missile tube aboard USS PATRICK HENRY. The PATRICK HENRY was fitted with sixteen tubes, each armed (initially) with the Polaris A-1 missile. She was later backfitted with the improved Polaris A-3 missile. (National Archives)

Crewmen swing a Mk 16 Mod 6 torpedo from a harbor utility craft over to the USS PATRICK HENRY for loading through the torpedo loading trunk at Holy Loch, Scotland during 1962. The Mk 16 was eventually replaced by the Mk 48 torpedo. (National Archives)

The THEODORE ROOSEVELT made her first operational patrol out of Charleston, South Carolina on 19 July 1961 carrying sixteen Polaris A-1 missiles. All GEORGE WASHINGTON class subs were also fitted with six bow mounted torpedo tubes, since they started out as an attack sub design (Navy)

The USS THEODORE ROOSEVELT (SSBN 600) rounds North Island as she enters San Diego Harbor on 22 February 1961, one week following her commissioning. The THEODORE ROOSEVELT was built by Mare Island Shipyard, California some 500 miles from San Diego. The THEODORE ROOSEVELT was armed with Polaris A-1 missiles. (Navy)

The ABRAHAM LINCOLN (SSBN 602) heads out to sea for trials during 1960. The ABRAHAM LINCOLN was built by the Portsmouth Naval Shipyard and was commissioned on 8 March 1961. The ABRAHAM LINCOLN was finished in the Black and Dark Gray scheme, the Dark Gray being applied to the missile deck side superstructure. (Portsmouth Naval Shipyard)

The USS ROBERT E. LEE (SSBN 601) at sea prior to sailing to Cape Canaveral to launch a Polaris missile. The ROBERT E. LEE made her first operational patrol on 2 May 1961 and on 25 February 1982 she offloaded her Polaris A-3 missiles. She was the last operational GEORGE WASHINGTON class FBM submarine. (Navy)

The USS ABRAHAM LINCOLN undergoes repair and refit in the LOS ALAMOS (AFDB-7), a large floating dry dock at Site One, Holy Loch, Scotland during March of 1963. The LOS ALAMOS served as Holy Loch's only dry dock facility for over thirty years. (Navy)

ETHAN ALLEN Class

Following the lead of the GEORGE WASHINGTON class, all five ships in the ETHAN ALLEN Class were named after famous Americans. The first and third ship in the class, USS ETHAN ALLEN (SSBN 608) and USS THOMAS A. EDISON (SSBN 610), were built on the ways at Electric Boat on the Thames River, Groton, CT. The second, forth and fifth subs, USS SAM HOUSTON (SSBN 609), USS JOHN MARSHALL (SSBN 611) and USS THOMAS JEFFERSON (SSBN 618), were built by Newport News Shipbuilding on the James River, Newport News, Virginia. They were launched and commissioned from 1961 through early 1962 and made their first deterrent patrols in late 1962 and early 1963 from Charleston, South Carolina. All ships received their basic missile load outs at Chareston.

The ETHAN ALLEN Class were armed with sixteen Polaris A-2 (UGM-27B) SLBMs with a range of 1,700 miles, a 320 mile range improvement over the Polaris A-1. As in the GEORGE WASHINGTON Class the MK 80 missile fire control system was employed to fire the missiles. During 1965 and 1966 the subs of the ETHAN ALLEN Class were backfitted with the improved Polaris A-3 (UGM-27C) missile and gas generator/steam ejection missile launch system.

The ETHAN ALLEN Class were the first fleet ballistic missile submarines designed from the outset to launch ballistic missiles. They were constructed using submarine design SCB-180. The design employed a THRESHER (SSN 593) type deep diving hull that was constructed of Hy 80 steel. The design would enable the ETHAN ALLEN class to dive deeper than the GEORGE WASHINGTON Class. The hull was 410 feet long with a beam of thirty-three feet. Surface displacement was 6,955 tons and submerged displacement was 7,880 tons.

The ETHAN ALLEN Class was powered by the Westinghouse S5W water cooled reactor. ETHAN ALLEN, SAM HOUSTON and THOMAS A. EDISON were fitted with Westinghouse geared turbines while the JOHN MARSHALL and THOMAS JEFFERSON were fitted with General Electric turbines. As in all other ballistic missile submarines, these ships used a seven blade screw. The 15,000 horse power reactor provided a top speed of twenty plus knots while submerged.

The ETHAN ALLEN Class was fitted with four 21 inch torpedo tubes in the bow for a purely defensive role and they initially carried the Mk 16 Mod 6 or Mk 37 electric torpedo. In 1974 the Mk 48 multi-purpose torpedo became available and it replaced the earlier torpedoes as the standard torpedo carried on all FBM submarines. The torpedo fire control fitted was the Mark 112 Mod 2 system that tied in directly with the onboard sonar and the Mark 2 Mod 3 Ships Inertial Navigation System (SINS).

The ETHAN ALLEN Class was also known as the 608 Class and they operated in the Atlantic and Mediterranean from the forward operating base at Holy Loch, Scotland until the mid-1970s when the five ships were systematically redeployed to the Pacific, operating out of Apra Harbor, Guam. By the time the Pacific redeployment took place, all of the class had been backfitted with the improved Polaris A-3T missile.

The 608 Class continued to operate in the Pacific on deterrent patrols until 1981 when all five ships of the class were redesignated and operated as attack submaries (SSNs). As SSNs their missiles and missile fire control systems were removed. In the case of the SAM HOUSTON and JOHN MARSHALL they would be used in the special operations role for many years. They were both fitted with Dry Deck Shelters (DDS) that served as housings for SEAL Team swimmer vehicles. The DDS also served as ingress/egress points for the SEAL Teams. The two DDS canisters were fitted aft of the sail on the upper decking of the two subs. As of early 1992, the JOHN MARSHALL was still operating in the Atlantic fleet and the SAM HOUSTON in the Pacific.

The GEORGE WASHINGTON (598) and ETHAN ALLEN (608) Classes were not upgraded to the Poseidon missile when it became available since their useful lives as FBM submarines had come to an end, with some of the class having been in service for over 20 years.

USS GEORGE WASHINGTON

Length: 382 Feet

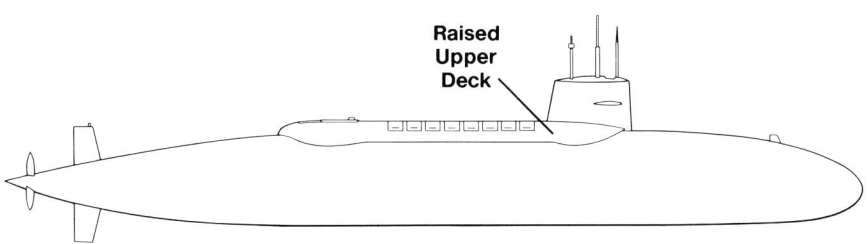

USS ETHAN ALLEN

Length: 410 Feet

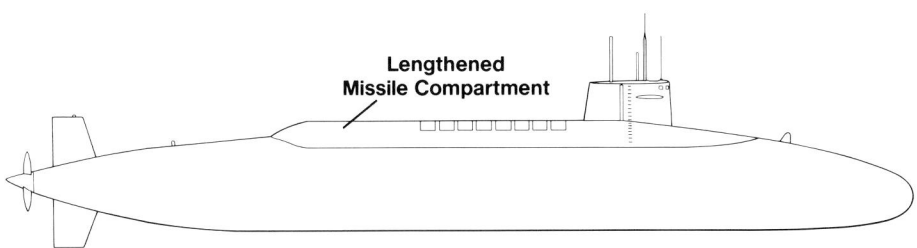

The USS ETHAN ALLEN (SSBN 608) underway during her sea trials held in 1961. The ETHAN ALLEN was built by the Electric Boat Division of General Dynamics Corporation and was launched on 22 November 1960, the first of a new class of FBM submarines. ETHAN ALLEN made her first operational patrol on 26 June 1962 armed with the Polaris A-2 missiles. (Electric Boat)

The captain of the USS ETHAN ALLEN communicates his orders to the missile control center during a launch exercise. The captain is standing next to one of the two onboard periscopes that are used for air and surface observations. (National Archives)

A Torpedoman rolls a Mk 16 Torpedo into position in the torpedo room of the USS ETHAN ALLEN in preparation for stowing. The ETHAN ALLEN was fitted with four 21 inch torpedo tubes mounted in the bow which differed from the earlier GEORGE WASHINGTON Class which carried six tubes. (National Archives)

The first Polaris A-2 launch was made by USS ETHAN ALLEN on 23 October 1961 while submerged off the coast of Cape Canaveral. The following June, the ETHAN ALLEN departed Charleston Harbor on her first operational patrol. The Polaris A-2 had a range of 1,700 miles and was armed with a 500 KT W-47 thermonuclear weapon. (Lockheed)

The USS SAM HOUSTON (SSBN 609) underway out of Apra Harbor, Guam on 29 January 1979. The SAM HOUSTON was the first Polaris submarine to be assigned to the Mediterranean patrol area during October of 1962. On her first Med patrol she visited Izmir, Turkey, the first visit to a foreign port by an FBM sub. (Navy)

Officers and men of the deck watch man the bridge on USS ETHAN ALLEN during 1964. The periscope, radar and radio antennas are extended for use in the surface watch. The officer on the left has his hand on a signal lamp that is used for surface communications between ships. (National Archives)

The USS SAM HOUSTON (SSBN 609) loads a Polaris A-2 missile while pier side during 1965. The missile is in a protective loading shell designed to protect the soft sides of the missile from damage during loading and unloading. The A-2 missiles were eventually replaced by the more powerful and longer ranged A-3 missile system. (National Archives)

The THOMAS A. EDISON (SSBN 610) slides down the ways at Electric Boat on 15 June 1961. The Electric Boat Division of General Dynamics has built more fleet ballistic missile submarines than any other company. Electric Boat is located on the Thames River, Groton, Connecticut. (Electric Boat)

President John F. Kennedy at the periscope of the THOMAS A. EDISON during a visit aboard on 14 April 1962. President Kennedy was a decorated Naval officer, having skippered the PT 109 in the Pacific during World War II. Both PT 109 and the EDISON were built by divisions of Electric Boat. (Navy via Lockheed)

USS JOHN MARSHALL (SSBN 611), underway on her sea trials in 1961, reveals the smooth upper hull design that replaced the raised hull of the GEORGE WASHINGTON Class. Telemetry mast braces were fitted to the sides of the sail in preparation for launching a Polaris A-2 missile from the Atlantic test facility, Cape Canaveral, Florida. (Navy)

The THOMAS JEFFERSON (SSBN 618) was the last submarine of the ETHAN ALLEN class. She made her first operational patrol on 28 October 1963 from Charleston, South Carolina. The THOMAS JEFFERSON was backfitted with the improved Polaris A-3 missile system during her second overhaul in 1975. (Navy)

The JOHN MARSHALL (SSBN 611) was reconfigured as an SSN during 1985. The two containers on the aft weather deck are called Dry Deck Shelters (DDS) and are used to transport Navy SEAL team swimmer vehicles and their equipment. The JOHN MARSHALL is attached to the Atlantic fleet and was recently involved in the Persian Gulf War inserting SEAL teams into Iraq. (Navy)

LAFAYETTE Class

On 8 July 1960, President John F. Kennedy authorized the construction of a new class of FBM submarine to be named the LAFAYETTE (SSBN 616) Class. The first five (of nine) of the class were authorized in 1960 and the balance on 29 January 1961. President Kennedy, in an unprecedented move, accelerated the FBM construction program partly to offset Soviet Submarine construction, but also to bolster our nuclear deterrent capability. The 1961 authorization bill also provided for the construction of the FBM submarine tender USS HOLLAND (AS-32), the first purpose built fleet ballistic missile submarine tender.

The LAFAYETTE (616) Class of submarines were built using BUSHIPS design number SCB-216 that provided for a hull length of 425 feet and a beam of thirty-three feet, the same beam of the two earlier classes of FBM subs. Maximum draft was thirty-two feet, surface displacement rose to 7,310 tons and submerged displacement was 8,260 tons. Although hull length was increased, no additional crew members were accommodated, but overall crew space was increased making the LAFAYETTE (or 616) Class more habitable on long patrols. The 616 Class was manned by fifteen Officers and 130 enlisted men. As in all previous classes, all crew, with the exception of the Captain and the Executive Officer, were tripled bunked.

For defense, the subs were fitted with four 21 inch Mark 65 torpedo tubes in the bow. The FBM submarine is not a hunter and relies on being quiet for their survival; the torpedoes would be a last resort weapon. Torpedo fire control was provided by the Mark 113 fire control system. The BQS-4 active/passive sonar was the same basic system that was installed in the SKIPJACK (SSN 587) Class high speed nuclear attack submarines.

As in the two earlier classes (598 and 608), the LAFAYETTE Class was also fitted with the Westinghouse S5W water nuclear reactor that produced 15,000 horse power, providing a maximum submerged speed of over 20 knots. Three types of geared turbines were fitted: the USS LAFAYETTE (SSBN 616), USS ALEXANDER HAMILTON (617), USS ANDREW JACKSON (619), USS JOHN ADAMS (620), and USS WOODROW WILSON (624) were fitted with two General Electric geared turbines, USS NATHAN HALE (623) was fitted with a DeLaval turbine, while the USS JAMES MONROE (622), USS HENRY CLAY (625) and USS DANIEL WEBSTER (626) were fitted with Westinghouse geared turbines.

The LAFAYETTE Class were originally built to handle the larger and longer range Poseidon C-3 missile system, but the missile system was not available for installation when the subs were constructed. As a result, the Polaris A-2 missile system was fitted with the intention to backfit the Poseidon at a later date. The USS LAFAYETTE departed Charleston on 4 January 1964, becoming the first FBM submarine to be stationed with Submarine Squadron 16 at Rota, Spain. The USS DANIEL WEBSTER was the last of the LAFAYETTE class and she was fitted with the Polaris A-3P and went on her first deterrent patrol on 26 September 1964.

The DANIEL WEBSTER (SSBN 626) was also selected to be modified with bow diving planes on a bow protrusion. This was a departure from the usual placement of the diving planes on the sail and she was the only FBM to be modified. In the event, the bow mounted planes were not successful and were eventually moved to the sail during one of her refit periods.

The LAFAYETTE Class had a direct influence on the British FBM submarine program. Great Britain's four RESOLUTION Class SSBNs are the same overall size and design as the LAFAYETTEs, and employed the bow mounted diving planes (common to all UK submarines) and the Aerojet/Hercules Polaris A-3 missile system and missile fire control system.

During the mid 1970s, when the Poseidon system became available, all of the LAFAYETTE Class FBMs were backfitted with these more powerful and longer range mis-

Lafayette Class

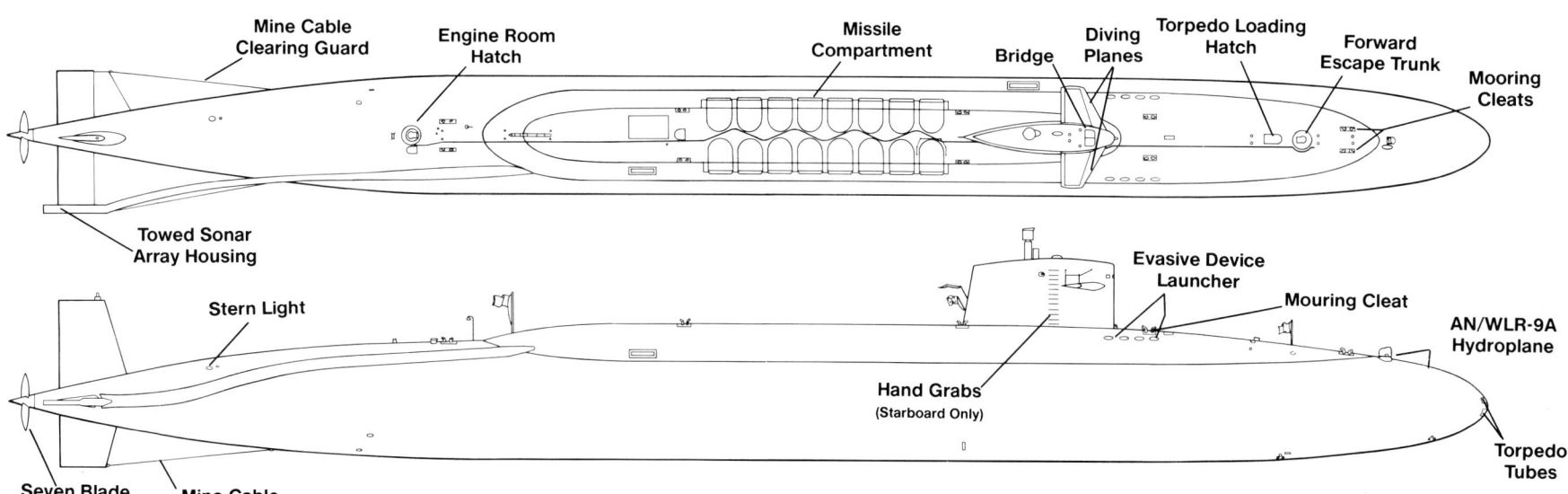

siles. The conversion and refit took two years to complete and included the removal of the missile tube liners and replacing them with larger diameter liners. The missile fire control system was also upgraded with the Mark 88 system replacing the earlier Mark 84. The conversions were undertaken during the regular overhaul period and were completed by five different shipyards.

Electric Boat built the lead ship USS LAFAYETTE (616), along with SSBN 617 and 623. Newport News Shipbuilding built SSBN 619, 622 and 625. Portsmouth Naval Shipyard built SSBN 620 and Mare Island constructed SSBN 624. It took two years from the first launching in 1962 until the last ship was commissioned in 1964.

To comply with the provisions of the Salt I Treaty, USS NATHAN HALE was decommissioned on 11 February 1988 (she had essentially reached her useful life span of 25 years). As in other earlier classes, she was dismantled and disposed of after all sensitive missile and reactor equipment was removed. This left eight operational LAFAYETTE Class FBMs. As the new OHIO Class become operational, the remaining LAFAYETTEs will either be decommissioned or operated as SSNs before decommissioning and retirement.

Beginning in 1983, during their third overhaul period, the LAFAYETTE, ALEXANDER HAMILTON and WOODROW WILSON were back fitted with the Trident I C-4, the only three of the LAFAYETTE Class to be so modified. The balance of the class were decommissioned between 1988 to 1990. The DANIEL WEBSTER (626) was designated a moored training ship (MTS 626) during 1990 and will be stationed at Charleston Naval Submarine Base. The USS SAM RAYBURN (SSBN 635) was also decommissioned and turned into a floating training ship. Other SSBNs may also be configured to provide reactor prototype training to all officers and enlisted going through nuclear training. The moored training ships are replacing the land based training facilities to give a more realistic training atmosphere.

The LAFAYETTE Class originally contained nineteen ships, but was broken into two classes during late 1980 to distinguish between the earlier nine LAFAYETTE (SSBN 616/617, 619-626) Class FBMs and the ten newer modified JAMES MADISON (SSBN 627-636) class.

To comply with the provisions of the START Treaty (Strategic Arms Reduction Treaty) the ALEXANDER HAMILTON and WOODROW WILSON will be inactivated and all weapon systems removed by July of 1992. The USS LAFAYETTE was decommissioned in 1990.

USS LAFAYETTE (SSBN 616) off the coast of Norfolk, Virginia during December 1968. The deck officer and lookout crew are manning the sail area as the sub makes its way through the water at 15 knots. The LAFAYETTE served until 1991 when she was decommissioned. (Navy)

The USS ALEXANDER HAMILTON (SSBN 617) underway at very low speed during 1963. ALEXANDER HAMILTON was built by Electric Boat and departed on her first deterrent patrol out of Charleston, South Carolina on 16 March 1964 with a full load of Polaris A-2 Missiles. (Navy)

USS LAFAYETTE (SSBN 616), on sea trials in the Atlantic Ocean, was escorted by three SH-3A Sea King Helicopters from Helicopter Antisubmarine Squadron Nine (HS-9). The LAFAYETTE was the lead boat of its class and was built by Electric Boat, being launched on 8 May 1962. (National Archives)

With safety line rigged, USS ANDREW JACKSON (SSBN 619) moves at high speed during her sea trials held in June of 1963. The ANDREW JACKSON was built by Mare Island Naval Shipyard, Vallejo, California and was assigned to Submarine Squadron Sixteen, Charleston, South Carolina. (Navy)

USS JAMES MONROE (SSBN 622) operating on the surface during sea trials following her conversion and backfitting to the Polaris A-3 missile system. The vertical braces fitted to the aft sail area are for a telemetry mast which was to be fitted at Cape Canaveral (Cape Kennedy) for missile trials. The JAMES MONROE was decommissioned on 24 March 1989. (Navy)

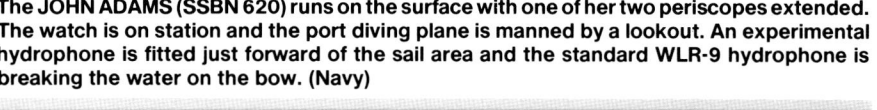

The JOHN ADAMS (SSBN 620) runs on the surface with one of her two periscopes extended. The watch is on station and the port diving plane is manned by a lookout. An experimental hydrophone is fitted just forward of the sail area and the standard WLR-9 hydrophone is breaking the water on the bow. (Navy)

USS NATHAN HALE (SSBN 623) is launched from the building ways at Electric Boat into the Thames River on 12 January 1963. NATHAN HALE departed Charleston, SC on 25 May 1964 on her first deterrent, armed with sixteen Polaris A-2 missiles. (Electric Boat)

The USS THEODORE ROOSEVELT (SSBN 600) at high speed on the surface. The ROOSEVELT was assigned to Submarine Squadron Fourteen (SUBRON-14) out of Holy Loch, Scotland.

USS DANIEL WEBSTER (SSBN 626) was the only FBM submarine to be outfitted with bow mounted diving planes.

The USS THOMAS JEFFERSON (SSBN 618) was an ETHAN ALLEN Class FBM. The vertical support on the sail was used to hold a telemetry mast during practice missile firings.

USS CASIMIR PULASKI (SSBN 633), is a JAMES MADISON Class FBM submarine. After a long period at sea the Red Oxide paint will turn a very dark Green color.

A ballistic missile is loaded into missile tube fifteen aboard the USS FRANCIS SCOTT KEY (SSBN 657).

White exhaust smoke comes out of the diesel engine exhaust ports on the sail of USS ALASKA (SSBN 732) during tests of the snorkel and diesel engine.

USS NATHAN HALE at sea during trials before sailing to Cape Canaveral for a practice launch of a Polaris A-2 missile. The NATHAN HALE was backfitted with the Polaris A-3 and the Poseidon C-3 missile systems during overhaul periods and was finally decommissioned in 1986 after serving twenty-three years. (Navy)

The USS HENRY CLAY (SSBN 625) in the launching dock at Newport News Shipbuilding prior to her commissioning on 30 November 1962. The seven blade screw, aft diving planes and rudder are visible. The screw design was classified until just recently. (Navy)

The USS WOODROW WILSON (SSBN 624) underway off the coast of South Carolina in July 1977. Twelve of her sixteen missile doors are in the open position and the launch tube upper seals are visible. The missile tubes were fitted with the Poseidon C-3 missiles. (Navy)

USS HENRY CLAY runs on the surface with her periscope extended. The extendable devices are painted Gray with Dark Gray splotches to break up their outline. (Navy)

With the bow mounted diving planes fitted, commissioning ceremonies were held for USS DANIEL WEBSTER on 9 April 1964. In the event, the bow planes offered no improvement in control and they were later removed and replaced by standard sail mounted planes during her first overhaul period in 1969. (Electric Boat)

Bow Mounted Diving Planes

USS DANIEL WEBSTER

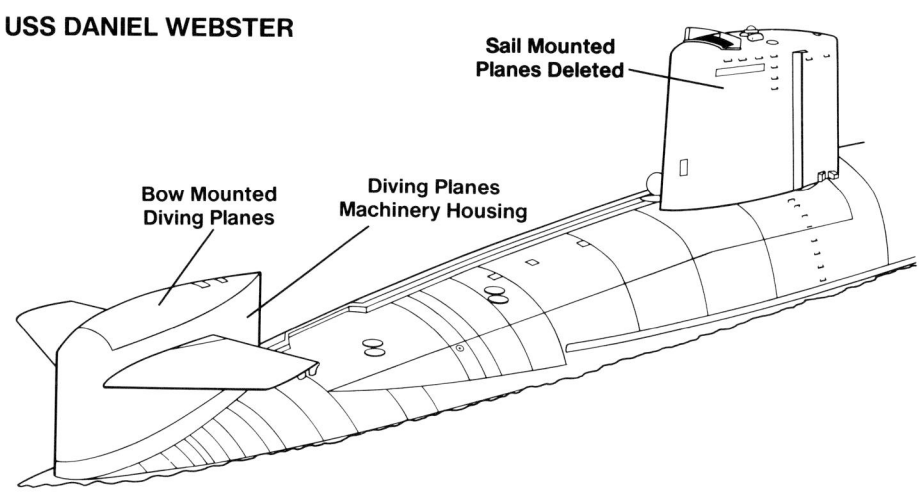

The DANIEL WEBSTER (SSBN 626) slides down the ways at Electric Boat on 27 April 1963. The DANIEL WEBSTER was then moved to a refit dry dock for the installation of experimental bow mounted diving planes. Commissioning ceremonies took place on 9 April 1964, just over a year later. (Electric Boat)

The USS DANIEL WEBSTER at sea during tests of the bow mounted diving planes in 1964. The bow planes increased water resistance, lowering her top speed. The planes did reduce the effects of porpoising, but the disadvantages outweighed the advantages and they were removed. (Navy)

The DANIEL WEBSTER entering Charleston, SC in February of 1990 prior to her conversion to the Navy's second moored training ship. Once converted she was redesignated as (MTS 626). The DANIEL WEBSTER served for over twenty-seven years and was the first of the LAFAYETTE Class to be backfitted with the Poseidon missile system. (Navy)

The DANIEL WEBSTER traverses in Holy Loch, Scotland during 1990 with a temporary radar antenna fitted to the sail. Fog could quickly build up in the Loch and a surface radar was essential for safe navigation. The surface watch is outfitted with cold weather gear indicating foul conditions. (Navy)

29

JAMES MADISON Class

On 19 July 1961, President John F. Kennedy authorized the construction of the 20th thru 29th SSBN. The subs were to be constructed using BUSHIPS submarine design SCB-216 Mod 3. Newport News was selected to construct the lead boat, USS JAMES MADISON (SSBN 627) as well as the USS JOHN C. CALHOUN (630), USS VON STUBEN (632) and USS SAM RAYBURN (635). Electric Boat was selected to build USS TECUMSEH (620), USS ULYSSES S. GRANT (631) and USS CASIMIR PULASKI (633). Mare Island built two of the class, USS DANIEL BOONE (629) and USS STONEWALL JACKSON (634), while Portsmouth constructed USS NATHANAEL GREENE (636).

All of the 627 Class were originally fitted with the Polaris A-3 missile system, but during their first overhaul period (between March of 1971 to April of 1972) the Poseidon C-3 missile system and Mark 88 fire control system were backfitted. During the period from October 1979 thru February 1982 DANIEL BOONE, JOHN C. CALHOUN and STONEWALL JACKSON were backfitted with the Trident I C-4 (UGM-96A) missile system. The JAMES MADISON, VON STUBEN and CASIMIR PULASKI were backfitted during their regular overhaul periods. DANIEL BOONE was the first 627 class to be backfitted with the Trident and she became operational on 6 September 1980 with the new missiles. The Trident backfit was not performed on the TECUMSEH, ULYSSES S. GRANT, SAM RAYBURN or NATHANAEL GREENE.

As it shared the same 216 submarine design as the 616 Class, the JAMES MADISON Class had a hull length of 425 feet, a beam of thirty-three feet and a draft of thirty-two feet. Displacement both surface and submerged increased to 7,320 and 8,240 tons respectively due mainly to equipment and machinery changes partially brought about by the USS TRESHER accident. Berthing also increased by two enlisted men (to 132) while officer strength remained at fifteen.

The 627 Class is powered by the Westinghouse S5W water cooled reactor, the same power plant that was used in the LAFAYETTE, ETHAN ALLEN and GEORGE WASHINGTON Class ships. The reactor produces 15,000 shaft horsepower and provides the power to the two geared turbines which drive a single seven blade screw. The 627 Class, like the 616 Class before it, has a rated speed of 20 plus knots submerged and a deep diving capability of well over 400 feet due to its THRESHER hull design. Tragically, the USS THRESHER was lost at sea with all hands on 10 April 1963 off the coast of New England during a deep diving test after overhaul. It was suspected that internal flooding caused THRESHER to go below crush depth and after the accident, new safety measures were incorporated in the construction of the 627 and subsequent classes of submarines. The move was undertaken by the U.S. Navy and submarine builders to insure that an accident of that type would never again happen to a U.S. Navy submarine.

All of the Trident I converted 627 Class FBMs have been assigned to Kings Bay Naval Submarine Base, Georgia; however, they must sail to Charleston, S.C. to have their missiles either loaded or unloaded since Charleston is the Atlantic Coast Polaris and Trident I missile handing facility. Kings Bay, Georgia is the Atlantic coast Strategic Weapons Facility (SWFLANT) for the Trident II D-5 missile system.

The 627 Class is fitted with four Mark 65 torpedo tubes, loaded with Mark 48 all purpose torpedoes. The Mark 48 can be either wire guided or operate independently using

The JAMES MADISON Class FBM submarine, USS TECUMSEH (SSBN 628), underway off the coast of Groton, CT during builders trials held on 22 June 1963. The TECUMSEH carries the dark Gray hull side paint scheme that was standard during the early 1960s. The TECUMSEH was built by Electric Boat and was commissioned on 29 May 1964. (Navy)

active/passive homing. The Mk 48 has a range of over twenty-three miles and can dive to over 3,000 feet (500 fathoms). The Mk 48 weighs 3,520 pounds with a 650 pound warhead. The Mark 113 Mod 9 fire control system is utilized for torpedo fire control.

The JAMES MADISON Class, like the LAFAYETTE Class before it, is provided with the Mk 2 Mod 4 Ships Inertial Navigation System (SINS). The 608 Class was fitted with the Mod 3 while the 616 Class was fitted with the Mod 6 version. All of the submarines employ a satellite receiver to receive precise navigational information. The Trident I C-4 subsystem is an improvement of the basic Trident I design that was used in the 616 Class of SSBNs.

On 1 April 1986, the USS NATHANAEL GREENE ran aground while operating in the Irish Sea. The damage to the sub was such that repairs were not feasible and the decision was made to decommission her. By March of 1987, the decision was made to dismantle the USS SAM RAYBURN (SSBN 635). She was deactivated, decommissioned and converted into the first FBM submarine moored training ship (MTS 635).

The USS TECUMSEH and the USS ULYSSES S. GRANT were scheduled to be deactivated by July of 1992 to comply with the joint U.S./Soviet START Treaty. The remaining members of the class will serve on and will be taken off line as the newer OHIO Class FBMs are commissioned and brought to Kings Bay to start their deterrent patrols.

Crewmen of the USS DANIEL BOONE prepare the weather decks for diving by securing all ladders, hoses and flags. The DANIEL BOONE had just left a port call at Roosevelt Roads, Puerto Rico in October of 1970 and was about to resume her patrol. (Navy)

The USS JAMES MADISON (SSBN 627) cruises at high speed on the surface. The JAMES MADISON was originally part of the LAFAYETTE Class, but internal equipment changes led them to be designated as a new class of boats. The JAMES MADISON was built by Newport News Shipbuilding in Virginia. (Navy)

The USS JOHN C. CALHOUN (SSBN 630) tied up to the port side of USS CANOPUS (AS 34) at Kings Bay Naval Submarine Base, GA on 2 January 1992. The JOHN C. CALHOUN was transferred to Kings Bay from Holy Loch, Scotland when that base was deactivated during early 1992. (A. Adcock IV)

The JOHN C. CALHOUN in the Atlantic prior to her arrival at Cape Canaveral for a practice launch of a Polaris A-3 missile. An FM antenna and telemetry antenna braces are fitted to the sail area. The hull number, 630, will be painted out before she goes on her first patrol. (Navy)

The USS CASIMIR PULASKI pier side at the Layberth, Naval Submarine Base, Kings Bay, Georgia on 2 January 1992. She is preparing to go to sea on another seventy day patrol in the Atlantic area. The CASIMIR PULASKI was armed with sixteen Trident C-4 missiles with a 4,000 mile range. (A. Adcock IV)

The USS VON STUBEN cruises on the surface off the coast of Virginia during builders trials (1964). The VON STUBEN was assigned to Submarine Group Six, at Charleston, South Carolina and made her first deterrent patrol on 28 March 1965, armed with a full load of sixteen Polaris A-3 missiles (Navy)

The number two torpedo tube of the USS CASIMIR PULASKI was loaded with a warshot (live) Mark 48 dual purpose torpedo. All JAMES MADISON Class FBM submarines are fitted with four Mk 65 torpedo tubes in the bow. The whited out area covers a classified pressure gage on the torpedo tube door. (A. Adcock IV)

The USS CASIMIR PULASKI sits in the covered dock/drydock area at the Trident Refit Facility, Kings Bay, Georgia. The large structure in the background is the Explosive Handling Wharf (EHW) used to load and unload Trident missiles. (Navy via CDR J.E. Teske)

The USS CASIMIR PULASKI sails past Fort Clinch, Florida as she traverses the St Mary's River to the Atlantic Ocean on an operational patrol. The CASIMIR PULASKI was originally fitted with the Polaris A-3, but was backfitted first with the Poseidon C-3 and then with the Trident C-4 (Navy via CDR J.E. Teske)

The sail (Fairwater) area on the CASIMIR PULASKI shows the temporary windshield that is fitted for surface operations. The windshield folds for storage in the lower sail area. A handrail is also fitted to the upper sail area for use by the surface watch once the sub is under way. (Al Adcock IV)

A Mk 48 Torpedo is loaded through the torpedo loading trunk of the USS STONEWALL JACKSON (SSBN 634). The Mk 48 has a range of twenty-three miles and carries a 650 pound warhead. The STONEWALL JACKSON was assigned to Submarine Squadron 17 Bangor, Washington and made her first operational patrol on 9 April 1965. (National Archives)

The eight starboard missile tube doors are open on the USS SAM RAYBURN revealing the pre-Army/Navy football game message — "Beat Army." The snorkel is extended from the aft sail area. (U S Navy)

The USS STONEWALL JACKSON (SSBN 634) sails off of Oahu, Hawaii on 12 October 1964 during her shakedown cruise prior to being assigned to Naval Submarine Base Bangor, Washington. The STONEWALL JACKSON now serves with Atlantic Fleet and is armed with sixteen Trident C-4 missiles. (Navy)

Work on the missile tubes and doors proceeds just one month from the launching of the USS NATHANAEL GREENE in 1964. The safety track can be seen between the missile tube doors. The safety track is used by deck crews during deck operations while at sea. (Portsmouth Naval Shipyard)

The USS NATHANAEL GREENE (SSBN 636) slides into the water at the Portsmouth Naval Shipyard, Kittery, Maine on 12 May 1964. All of the officers and enlisted personnel are called "Plank Owners" since they helped build and launch the ship. The NATHANAEL GREENE successfully launched a Polaris missile from the surface on 15 March 1965. (Portsmouth Naval Shipyard)

The USS NATHANAEL GREENE runs on the surface during builders trials. During April of 1986 the NATHANAEL GREENE ran aground in the Irish Sea severely damaging the hull. She was examined during May of 1986 and it was found that the damage to the hull was such that repairs were not feasible and she was scrapped. (Portsmouth Naval Shipyard)

BENJAMIN FRANKLIN Class

The BENJAMIN FRANKLIN (SSBN 640) class was basically a reengineered LAFAYETTE Class, utilizing the BUSHIPS sub design 216. The class was actually built in two different variants. The first six, USS BENJAMIN FRANKLIN (SSBN 640), USS SIMON BOLIVAR (641), USS KAMEHHAMEHA (642) USS GEORGE BANNCROFT (643), USS LEWIS AND CLARK (644) and USS JAMES K. POLK (645) were built using BUSHIPS design SCB 216 Mod 2; while the USS GEORGE C. MARSHALL (654), USS HENRY L. STIMSON (655), USS GEORGE WASHINGTON CARVER (656), USS FRANCIS SCOTT KEY (657), USS MARIANO G. VALLEJO (658) and USS WILL ROGERS (659) were built to the SCB 216 Mod 3 submarine design.

The SSBN 640 Class were built by three different builders: Electric Boat produced 640, 643, 645, 655, 657 and 659, Newport News Shipbuilding built 641, 644, 654 and 656, while Mare Island Naval Shipyard built two, SSBN 642 and 658. All of the class are powered by the 15,000 shaft horse power Westinghouse S5W high pressure, water cooled nuclear reactor. The SCB 216 Mod 2 design provided for very quite machinery. This was made possible by placing the geared turbines and related propeller shaft housing on resilient shock absorbing material that cushioned the shock of movement, helping to further reduce machinery noise. To further aid in noise reduction, cork and rubber panels were placed in areas of high noise. Performance figures remained the same as the 627 Class with a rated speed of 20 plus knots submerged.

Although the LAFAYETTE, JAMES MADISON and BENJAMIN FRANKLIN class look big on the outside, once you enter one of the hatches and go below decks you will find the quarters to be very close, with all space fully utilized. Triple bunking is the standard and the largest open area on the ship is the enlisted mess area. The medical facility is the size of four telephone booths and, in an emergency, the officers ward room would serve as the operating theater.

As in other members of the 616 and 627 Class FBMs, the BENJAMIN FRANKLIN (640) Class is fitted with four bow mounted Mark 65, 21 inch torpedo tubes that carry Mark 48 dual purpose torpedoes controlled by a Mark 113 Mod 9 torpedo fire control system.

The BENJAMIN FRANKLIN (640) Class were launched and commissioned with the Polaris A-3 (UGM-27C) ballistic missile, but during their first overhaul periods (from November of 1972 thru September of 1974) the ships were backfitted with the Poseidon C-3 (UGM-73A) and when the more powerful and longer range Trident I C-4 became available, these were also backfitted. USS BENJAMIN FRANKLIN, SIMON BOLIVAR and GEORGE BANCROFTS received theirs during their second overhaul, while the HENRY L. STIMSON, FRANCIS SCOTT KEY and MARIANO G. VALLEJO were backfitted pierside by a sub tender. The Trident backfit required an electronic upgrading to include navigational and satellite receiving systems. Portsmouth Naval Shipyard did the first Trident C-4 Backfit on the SIMON BOLIVAR beginning on 2 March 1979 and on 26 June 1981 she deployed from Charleston, South Carolina carrying a full load of sixteen Trident I C-4 (UGM-96A) missiles.

The 640 Class shared the SCB 216 hull design with the earlier 616 and 627 Class (425 foot length and thirty-three foot beam) and the bow contained an updated BQR-21 conformal sonar that featured Digital Multi-beam Steering (DIMUS). Later in their service careers some 640 Class were modified with twin vertical end plate stabilizers replacing the single tall vertical fin/rudder.

The USS BENJAMIN FRANKLIN (SSBN 640) underway near San Juan Bay, Puerto Rico during January 1966, three months after her commissioning ceremonies. The BENJAMIN FRANKLIN was the lead boat of her class and featured quieter machinery and a larger crew than earlier FBM submarines. The entire BENJAMIN FRANKLIN class was originally outfitted with Polaris A-3 missiles. (Navy)

All BENJAMIN FRANKLIN Class, as well as LAFAYETTE and JAMES MADISON Class submarines, are fitted with the BQR-15 or -17 towed sonar array depending on the year. The -15 was the early installation and the -17 the later upgraded unit. The sonar towed array is deployed on the starboard vertical stabilizer. The array is fitted to a long trailing tow cable that carries sensors that can listen for any hostile submarine or surface ship. The class is also fitted with various decoys such as the WLR-8 electronic countermeasure (ECM) decoy. The ECM decoy simulates the noise that various types of submarines would make. The 640 Class is also fitted with explosively deployed devices (EDD) that are fired from the center hull area. These mask the noise made by the submarine to enable it to escape from any potential enemy that might detect it.

All of the BENJAMIN FRANKLIN Class submarines are currently operating out of Kings Bay Naval Submarine Base, Georgia as their home port.

The KAMEHHAMEHA, LEWIS AND CLARK, JAMES K. POLK, GEORGE C. MARSHALL, GEORGE WASHINGTON CARVER and WILL ROGERS will be decommissioned and all missiles and missile systems removed to comply with recent nuclear reduction initiatives. This treaty called for reduction of a great majority of strategic weapons systems including the deployment of current and future inter-continental missile systems.

The forty-one submarines that originally made up the GEORGE WASHINGTON, ETHAN ALLEN, JAMES MADISON and BENJAMIN FRANKLIN Class FBMs represented a frantic build up of our nuclear underwater deterrent force brought on by the equally frantic build up of the Soviet sea and land forces. Events that began in the early 1990s attest to the awesome power that a submarine based nuclear deterrent force can bring to bear on unfriendly forces. Neither the United States of America nor the Soviets wanted to be the first to unleash the untold destruction carried on the FBMs and because of this the SSBN's role of nuclear deterrence was proven and their mission was truly accomplished.

The USS BENJAMIN FRANKLIN moored alongside the Trident Refit Wharf at Kings Bay Naval Submarine Base on 2 January 1992. The BENJAMIN FRANKLIN was modified with stern diving end plates replacing the vertical rudder. (A. Adcock IV)

Rudder/Fin Development

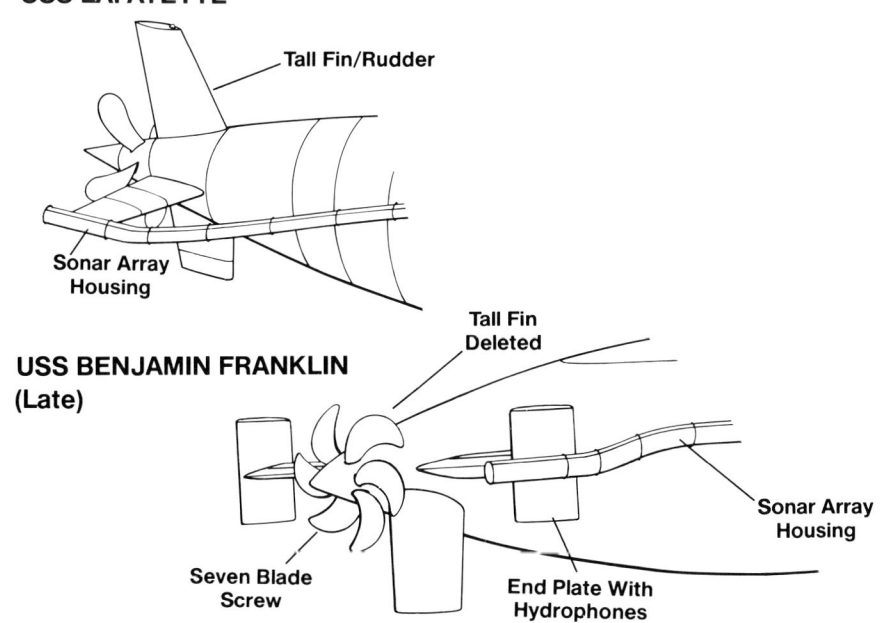

The USS SIMON BOLIVAR (SSBN 641) was built by Newport News Shipbuilding and was commissioned on 29 October 1965. She made her first deterrent patrol from Charleston, SC, on 27 April 1966 armed with a full load of Polaris A-3 missiles. (Navy)

The USS KAMEHAMEHA (SSBN 642) on the surface off the coast of Hawaii during 1965. The KAMEHAMEHA made her first operational patrol from Apra Harbor, Guam on 6 August 1966 while serving with Commander Submarine Squadron 15 (COMSUBRON-15, CSS-15). (Navy)

USS GEORGE C. MARSHALL (SSBN 654) operating in the ship channel off the coast of Virginia during early 1966. The GEORGE C. MARSHALL departed Charleston, SC on 25 October 1966 on her first operational patrol and was upgraded with the Poseidon missile system during her first overhaul period. (Navy)

The snorkel of the USS FRANCIS SCOTT KEY (SSBN 657) shows the Gray/Dark Gray mottle camouflage scheme employed to break up the outline of the extendables while at sea. The snorkel was a Dutch design that enabled a sub to operate just under the surface while it provides air to the crew and/or the diesel auxiliary engine. (National Archives)

The HENRY L. STIMSON (SSBN 655) carried an unusual paint scheme on the side sail and hull area during 1972. The ship was camouflaged in a Medium Gray to break up the contrast of the standard all Black scheme. The HENRY L. STIMSON made her first Atlantic patrol on 23 February 1967. (Navy)

Trailed by a tug, the USS WILL ROGERS (SSBN 659) enters Holy Loch, Scotland. The four holes on the hull superstructure contain Explosively Deployed Evasion Devices (EDED) (decoys) and the bow protrusion contains the WLA-9 hydrophone. The WILL ROGERS departed Holy Loch refit site on 9 November 1991, the last FBM submarine to use the base. (Navy)

The USS FRANCIS SCOTT KEY (SSBN 657) is maneuvered by tugs shortly after her launching ceremonies at the Electric Boat Division of General Dynamics at Groton, CT on 23 April 1966. The tugs will move her to her mooring site for the completion of her internal outfitting. (Navy)

The USS SIMON LAKE (AS 33) loads a Poseidon C-3 missile into the Number 14 missile tube aboard a BENJAMIN FRANKLIN Class FBM submarine at Holy Loch during 1987. The Poseidon C-3 had a range of 2,500 nautical miles and could carry ten W-68 thermonuclear warheads. (Lockheed)

OHIO Class

The most powerful and costly class of U.S Navy submarines is the OHIO Class FBM submarines. The U.S. Navy awarded a fixed price contract to the Electric Boat Division of General Dynamics on 25 July 1974 for the construction and testing of one Trident submarine. The contract included an option for three additional submarines. The first hull was originally assigned hull number SSBN 711, but on 21 February 1974 it was reassigned hull number SSBN 1. In the following April it was again changed to SSBN 726 to conform with the regular progression of submarine hull numbers.

On 10 April 1976 the keel laying ceremonies took place at Electric Boat with the wife of Senator Robert Taft Jr. (R. Ohio) serving as the sponsor for the USS OHIO (SSBN 726). The OHIO Class were the largest submarines ever built by any Western nation, surpassed only in size by the Soviet Navy's TYPHOON Class and then only in beam, as the lengths are approximately the same: the OHIO at 560 feet and the TYPHOON at 562 feet. They both are about the size of a World War II light cruiser.

The OHIO Class will eventually grow to eighteen, all having been built or authorized by 1992. The first Trident submarine USS OHIO (SSBN 726) was commissioned on 11 November 1981 with Mrs. Annie Glenn, wife of Senator John Glenn of Ohio, as sponsor. The OHIO was followed by the USS MICHIGAN (727), USS FLORIDA (728), USS GEORGIA (729), USS HENRY M. JACKSON (730), USS ALABAMA (731), USS ALASKA (732) and USS NEVADA (733). All eight of these ships are serving in the Pacific Fleet out of Naval Submarine Base Bangor, Washington. The USS TENNESSEE (734), USS PENNSYLVANIA (735), USS WEST VIRGINIA (736), and USS KENTUCKY (737) are all commissioned and serving with the Atlantic Active Fleet, based at the Naval Submarine base, Kings Bay, Georgia. The USS MARYLAND (738) has been commissioned and in early 1992 was going through her workups in preparation for her Demonstration and Shakedown (DASO) cruise. This cruise will involve firing a Trident II missile from the Eastern test range off Cape Canaveral, Florida. The NEBRASKA (739), RHODE ISLAND (740), MAINE (741) and WYOMING (742) are in various stages of construction or outfitting. Hull number (743) has yet to be assigned a name (as of early 1992).

All of the OHIO Class ships have been produced at Electric Boat, a departure from the previous methods of letting up to four yards in on the construction process. The USS OHIO (726) was launched on 7 April 1979 after being on the final construction ways and assembly building for just under three years. It would be another two and a half years before commissioning ceremonies would take place. There were many reasons for the protracted time in construction, but one of the major reasons was the General Electric reactor turbines. It was discovered that some of the blades were potentially flawed and new turbine rotors had to be installed. Additionally, various changes in design and the steep learning curve involved in building the first of a totally new class of ships contributed significantly to the delays.

The OHIO Class were built using BUSHIPS design number SCB 304 and all are powered by a General Electric S8G pressurized water cooled nuclear reactor that produces over 35,000 equivalent shaft horsepower (SHP). The reactor provides steam for the Westinghouse geared turbines that drive a single seven blade screw. An auxiliary Fairbanks Morse diesel provides power for maneuvering in the event of a loss of nuclear reactor power. A snorkel is fitted in the aft upper sail area to provide fresh air to the crew or air for the diesel engine when at periscope depth. Performance figures for the OHIO are again a rated submerged speed of 20 plus knots and a maximum diving depth of 400 plus feet.

The OHIO Class is 560 feet in length and has a maximum beam of 42 feet. The extra beam width over the earlier FBM classes was determined by the size of the General Electric S8G reactor and the larger size of the Trident II D-5 missile. The maximum draft is 35.5 feet at the keel. The OHIOs have a surface displacement of 16,600 tons and a submerged displacement of 18,750 tons. The hull was built using a modular form of construction. Forty-two foot diameter cylinders were produced at Quonset Point, Rhode Island and shipped to Electric Boat for assembly. The cylinders were placed in large jigs and welded together, thus forming a long cylindrical submarine.

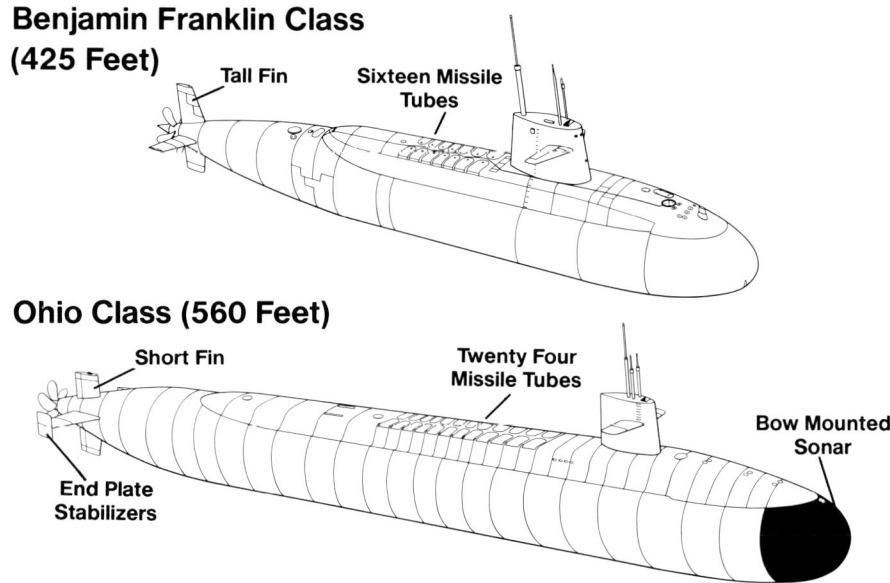

Benjamin Franklin Class (425 Feet)

Ohio Class (560 Feet)

On 22 April 1978, the first Trident ballistic missile submarine USS OHIO (SSBN 726), was rolled out of the assembly building and onto a waterfront pier at the Electric Boat Division of General Dynamics. Here the 560 foot long submarine will undergo final assembly and testing prior to being launched (7 April 1979). (Navy)

The first eight ships in the OHIO Class (726-733) were launched and fitted with the Trident I C-4 (UGM 96A) ballistic missile system. All of the OHIO Class have twenty-four missile tubes located aft of the sail arranged in two rows of twelve. From the TENNESSEE (734) and beyond all have been fitted with the Trident II D-5 (UGM 133) ballistic missile system. It was originally planned that all of the earlier (726-733) Class would be backfitted to the Trident II D-5 by the year 2000, but with the current state of world affairs the conversion may not take place. The D-5 is the most powerful submarine launched ballistic missile ever carried by any Navy. It features stellar and inertial navigation and can be armed with up to fourteen W-87 500 KT thermonuclear weapons per missile, housed in Mk 500 re-entry vehicles. The weapons system has a CEP (Circular Error of Probability) of 400 feet; this means after traveling over 4,000 miles that the warhead will hit an area within 400 feet of the designated target.

The missile load of one OHIO Class submarine could destroy as many as 336 independent targets. In actual deployment, the Trident II D-5 would only be loaded with a maximum of eight warheads and that would limit its range to 4,000 miles. The D-5 has a maximum range of over 6,000 miles, although range is reduced proportionally to the number of warheads fitted to each missile.

The OHIO Class are fitted with four decks (levels). The top level under the sail houses the Navigation Center, Command and Control Center, Sonar Room and Integrated Radio Room. The second level provides space for the Missile Control Center, ships offices and computer room. Level three contains the enlisted dining facilities, officers ward room, and chief petty officers (CPO) quarters. Level four houses the auxiliary machinery room number one and the torpedo room. The torpedo room is located midships between the bow and sail area and is fitted with four MK 68 torpedo tubes with the torpedoes being fired through long tubes. The location of the bow mounted sonar dictated the placement of the torpedo room. The spaces below level four are used to house the ship's emergency battery. The aft one third of the ship is occupied by the reactor compartment and engine room. The middle third by the missile compartment and the forward one third by ships operations. Enlisted crew berthing is located on the third level of the missile compartment, probably the quietest place on the ship.

The eyes of a submerged submarine is its sonar suite, either onboard or in a towed array. The passive sonar on the OHIO Class is the BQQ 6, which is comprised of the BQS 13 passive, spherical array sonar for fire control, a BQR 25 conformal hydrophone array, and a towed sonar array. The towed array is the BQR 23 and it is located on the aft upper port side of the hull. Missile Fire Control (MFC) is the Mk 98 digital computerized system. The Mk 48 dual purpose torpedoes are controlled by the Mk 118 Mod 2 fire control system. Surface radar surveillance is provided by the BPS 15A antenna that telescopes out of the sail (it is used only when the submarine is on the surface). As in earlier classes of FBM submarines, two periscopes are fitted. Both perform the same function of air and surface observation and attack.

With a useful life of some thirty years, the OHIO Class will be in operation well past 2010 and on into the 21st century. As the world continues to disarm, it appears that the only class of fleet ballistic missile submarines that will remain operational with the U.S. Navy will be the OHIO Class.

Operational testing of the twenty-four missile tube doors of the OHIO during precommissioning activities at the Electric Boat docks, Groton, Connecticut. The safety track, used by deck crewmen during foul weather, is visible between the missile tube doors. (Navy)

The USS OHIO was commissioned on 11 November 1981. Then Vice President, George Bush, spoke at the ceremony and Annie Glenn, wife of Ohio Senator John Glenn, was the ship's sponsor. The sign Good Luck Ohio was displayed on the forth Trident submarine, USS GEORGIA (SSBN 729). (Navy)

A Trident C-4 missile is loaded aboard the USS OHIO at the dock area of Port Canaveral, Florida during January of 1982. After loading, the OHIO sailed to the Atlantic test range off Cape Canaveral in preparation for a DASO. A telemetry mast was temporarily fitted aft of the sail so the submarine could communicate with the range safety officer. (Navy)

The USS OHIO arrived at her new home port, Naval Submarine Base Bangor, Washington on 12 August 1982. On 6 September 1982, the OHIO completed her strategic missile loadout and was declared operational with CAPT Alton K. Thompson, commander of the Blue crew, in command. (Navy)

CAPT (now Rear Admiral) Arlington F. Campbell on the bridge of the USS OHIO. The OHIO was leaving Port Canaveral enroute to Panama and a transit of the Panama Canal on its way to Naval Submarine Base Bangor, Washington, her new home port. CAPT Campbell was the commander of the Gold Crew. (RADM A.F. Campbell)

The USS OHIO was maneuvered by the USS MISHAWAKA (YTB 764) and two other tugs in the harbor of the Naval Submarine Base Bangor. The OHIO was using her auxiliary diesel power plant for maneuvering as was evidenced by the smoke coming from the diesel exhausts on the rear of upper sail area. (Navy)

A Lieutenant looks through one of the periscopes aboard USS OHIO. OHIO Class FBMs have two identical periscopes that can be used for both surface attack and navigation. (Navy)

Crewmen man the control and steering section of the USS OHIO during sea trials held in November of 1981. The OHIO steering section, as in all other FBM submarines, is normally manned by two junior crewmen with a supervisor, freeing up more experienced crewmen to perform other important tasks. (Navy)

The second OHIO Class FBM was the USS MICHIGAN under construction at Electric Boat, Groton, Connecticut during April of 1979. The enormous size of the MICHIGAN can be judged by the vehicles and people near the submarine. The MICHIGAN displaces 18,700 tons submerged and carries twenty-four Trident C-4 missiles. (Navy)

The USS MICHIGAN undergoing inclining test on 6 May 1982 at Electric Boat Groton, Connecticut. Inclining tests are used to determine a submarines ability to right herself from a roll. The MICHIGAN made her first deterrent patrol on 14 August 1983. (Navy)

The USS FLORIDA (SSBN 728) moves down the Straits of Juan De Fuca on her way to Bangor. The FLORIDA was commissioned on 18 June 1983, the third Trident submarine on active service. She deployed on her first operational patrol on 11 May 1984. (Navy)

The USS MICHIGAN entering the Magnetic Silencing Facility (MSF), Naval Submarine Base Bangor, Washington soon after her arrival on 1 March 1983. All Navy submarines enter the MSF to be tested for magnetic emissions. (Navy)

The USS HENRY M. JACKSON (SSBN 730) inside the Magnetic Silencing Facility, Naval Submarine Base Bangor, Washington during May of 1985. The HENRY M. JACKSON was the only deviation from the practice of naming all Trident submarines after U. S. States. (Navy)

The USS ALASKA (SSBN 731) being maneuvered by three tugs in the Hood Canal, Washington during 1991. The crewmen are standing on a sail staging platform which was attached to the sail. The ALASKA was commissioned on 25 January 1986 and deployed on her first operational deterrent patrol on 10 December 1986. (Navy)

The USS TENNESSEE (SSBN 734) was the first Trident II submarine designed to accommodate the improved Trident D-5. The D-5 weighs over 130,000 pounds and has a range of over 4,000 nautical miles. The USS TENNESSEE was assigned to Submarine Squadron 20 (CSS 20) at Naval Submarine Base Kings Bay, GA. (Navy)

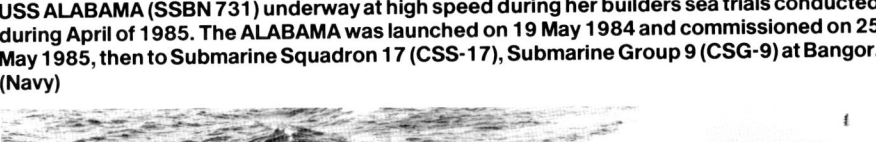

USS ALABAMA (SSBN 731) underway at high speed during her builders sea trials conducted during April of 1985. The ALABAMA was launched on 19 May 1984 and commissioned on 25 May 1985, then to Submarine Squadron 17 (CSS-17), Submarine Group 9 (CSG-9) at Bangor. (Navy)

Ship's officers stand at attention during colors ceremonies aboard the USS TENNESSEE soon after her arrival at Naval Submarine Base Kings Bay, Georgia on 15 January 1989. The TENNESSEE achieved initial operational capability on 23 March 1990 signaling the readiness of the Trident D-5 missile system. (Navy)

The USS TENNESSEE in the Explosive Handling Wharf, Strategic Weapons Facility, Kings Bay, Georgia. All of the TENNESSEE's missile tube doors are in the open position indicating that Trident missile loading will soon commence. (Lockheed)

The USS KENTUCKY (SSBN 737) moored to the Trident refit wharf at Kings Bay on 2 January 1992. The KENTUCKY was launched on 11 August 1990 and commissioned during 1991. A temporary radar antenna is fitted to the sail and will be removed once she reaches open sea and prepares to dive. (A. Adcock IV)

The sail staging platform attached to the sail of USS WEST VIRGINIA is used by refit crews to work on the various extendable devices on the sail area. The WEST VIRGINIA was the third Trident submarine to be assigned to Submarine Squadron 20 (CSS 20), at Kings Bay. (A. Adcock IV)

The USS PENNSYLVANIA (SSBN 735) at sea during builders trials in 1989 off the coast of Connecticut. The PENNSYLVANIA was commissioned on 9 September 1989 and was assigned to Submarine Squadron 20, at Kings Bay. The White painted area forward of the sail are reference marks for use by submarine rescue vessels and was removed once the sub becomes operational. (Navy)

The USS MARYLAND (SSBN 738) in the launching ways at Electric Boat awaiting launch ceremonies to commence on 10 August 1991. The USS NEBRASKA (SSBN 739) is still in the building stage on the construction pier. The OHIO Class is scheduled to eventually grow to eighteen ships. (Electric Boat)

A Trident II D-5 missile is loaded aboard the USS TENNESSEE during 1989 while moored in the Explosive Handling Wharf, Kings Bay. While the 130,000 pound missile is being loaded, a sufficient amount of water ballast must be pumped overboard to compensate for the weight. (Lockheed)

FBM Bases and Operations

In 1991 there were four FBM submarine bases, but by the end of 1992 that number was scheduled to be reduced to two; Kings Bay, Georgia and Bangor, Washington. Below is a listing of FBM bases, squadrons, operational bases and group:

SQUADRON	OPERATIONAL BASE	HOME PORT	GROUP
CSS-14	Holy Loch	New London, CT	CSG-2
CSS-15	Guam, Mariannas	Pearl Harbor, HI	CSP-5
CSS-16	Rota, Spain/Kings Bay	Charleston, SC	CSG-6
CSS-17	Bangor, Wa.	Bangor, WA	CSG-9
CSS-18	Charleston, SC	Charleston, SC	CSG-6
CSS-20	Kings Bay, GA	Kings Bay, GA	CSG-10

CSS-14 at Holy Loch was deactivated during February of 1992. The USS WILL ROGERS (SSBN-659) sailed out of Holy Loch, Scotland on 9 November 1991, marking the final FBM deterrent patrol from a foreign base. CSS-18 in Charleston is transferring its remaining SSBNs to CSS-16 and CSS-20 at Kings Bay, after which the squadron will be deactivated. CSS-15 at Guam was deactivated during 1981 and all SSBNs from CSS-16 were withdrawn from Rota, Spain and sent to Kings Bay. CSS-17 at Bangor Naval Submarine Base, Washington was activated in 1981 and as of late 1991 the squadron was comprised of eight early OHIO Class ships; the USS OHIO (SSBN 726), MICHIGAN (727) FLORIDA (728), GEORGIA (729), HENRY M. JACKSON (730) (formerly the RHODE ISLAND), ALABAMA (731) ALASKA (732) and NEVADA (733).

Kings Bay and Bangor are also the location of the Trident Training Facilities (TRITRAFAC). Each facility trains upwards of 25,000 officers and enlisted men each year. The training consists of time in the simulators that comprise the steering and diving section, command and control (attack center), navigation, damage control, missile and torpedo launch sections and most other aspects of the submarine. There is even a school for menu preparation, a very important consideration aboard a submarine. The Submarine School is at Groton, CT and it teaches basic submarine operations to both officer and enlisted students.

When an FBM sub leaves on a deterrent patrol it carries enough provisions and supplies for ninety days, but the usual patrol lasts about seventy days. Onboard a ballistic missile submarine the crew is fed four meals per day. The usual breakfast, lunch and supper (dinner), plus midnight rations called mid-rats. Mid-rats consist of sandwiches and salads and is basically for the crew that is pulling the graveyard or midnight watch, since the subs (like all Navy ships at sea) operate twenty-four hours a day. The food is prepared in one central mess (kitchen) and the enlisted men eat in shifts due to space limitations. The officers eat in the ward room, that also doubles as the medical operating room in an emergency. Earlier FBM subs had a crews mess that could seat about twenty-four, but the OHIO Class can accommodate about fifty. The serving is cafeteria style.

Space aboard a submarine is at a premium with all berthing areas in the sub triple bunked. The only exception being the Captain and Executive Officer, who are single bunked, and the Chief Of The Boat, who has a two bunk compartment (in some boats). The prize berthing areas are the missile compartment sections in the earlier classes, while in the OHIO Class all enlisted are berthed in the missile tube section, the quietest area of the subs. The Chief Petty Officers are provided berthing areas separate from other enlisted and the officers.

While at sea, and with the sub moving at depths of more than 400 feet, communications with land bases can be accomplished in four different ways. The sub can receive Airborne transmitted Very Low Frequency (AVLF) radio signals from two separate trailing wire antennas (one is 4,000 feet long and the other 26,000 feet long) that are trailed out by a Boeing E-6A Hermes, also called the Tacoma (Take charge and move out). The subs trailing receiving wire can also receive Extremely Low Frequency (ELF) transmissions from a land based ELF transmitters. The E-6A also has the capability to transmit and receive Very Low Frequency (VLF), High Frequency (HF) and Ultra High Frequency (UHF) transmissions. The submarines can receive a variety of transmissions from the ELF to UHF Utilizing extendable as well as trailing wire antennas.

Land to satellite to sub communications is handled by the Defense Information Systems Agency (DISA) and the Naval Computer and Telecommunications Command in Washington, D.C. DISA operates the various transmitter sites and satellites around the globe.

FBM submarines are manned by two separate crews designated the Blue and Gold. The two crews enable the subs to stay at sea a much greater percentage of time. In contrast, the Soviets operate their subs with one crew. This greatly reduces the time that any one sub can spend at sea. While the Blue or Gold crew is manning the sub, the opposite crew is either in training or on leave.

FBM subs have been built by four different shipyards. General Dynamics operates the Electric Boat Company (the old Holland Torpedo Boat Company) of Groton, CT. Electric Boat has produced the greatest number of FBM submarines and when production of the last OHIO Class sub is completed they will have produced a total of thirty-five FBM subs, over twice that of Newport News Shipbuilding and Drydock. Newport News is owned by Tenneco Corporation, a chemical and oil corporation, and has produced fifteen ships in all classes except the OHIO Class. Mare Island Naval Shipyard in Vallejo, California and Portsmouth Naval Shipyard in Kittery, Maine are both operated by the

The USS SIMON LAKE (AS 33) with four subs alongside in Holy Loch, Scotland. The SIMON LAKE was named for the submarine pioneer and designer/builder Simon Lake. The submarine tenders provide maintenance for the fleet ballistic missile submarines while in port. (Navy)

Navy. Mare Island produced six ships in four classes (no OHIO or ETHAN ALLEN Class) while Portsmouth built three ships, one each in the GEORGE WASHINGTON, LAFAYETTE and JAMES MADISON Class.

While at sea the interior lighting on the sub changes depending on the hour of day and the particular compartment of the ship that you are in. From sunset to sunrise the sub can be rigged for Red while near the surface and rigged for Gray or Black while on the surface to prevent any light from escaping through the periscope or an open hatch. The sonar room is rigged for Blue, actually a Blue-Green color that enhances the operators vision on the various sonar screens.

The interior of the early FBM subs was painted in various shades of Gray, but passageways are panelled in a flame retardant formica type of material. Heads and kitchen areas are constructed of stainless steel to help reduce clean up times. Ward rooms and enlisted mess areas are painted or panelled usually depicting a theme. The enlisted mess area aboard the KENTUCKY is called the Blue Grass Inn and the one aboard the CASIMIR PULASKI is decorated in the theme of an ancient sailing ship, complete with lanterns. The reason for the departure from the normal dining facilities aboard the submarines is to try and make at least one area pleasant and an enjoyable place to eat, train and socialize.

Color also plays an important part in depth perception, so various areas of the subs are painted in brilliant shades of Blue and Orange. The missile tubes in the Tridents (OHIO Class) are painted in various shades of Orange to aid in retaining depth perception while onboard, while the enlisted mess is brilliant Blue and Orange.

All U.S. Navy FBM submarines are painted in a pure soft Black non-fouling paint from the water line and above. There is a non-skid surface on the top side of the hull that extends about one-quarter down each side from centerline. The non-fouling painted surfaces are extremely slippery and great care must be taken by crew members to stay on the non-skid surfaces. The area between the waterline and the hull side centerline is painted in a very dark purple anti-fouling paint. The paint contains some copper compounds that turn the paint almost Black after some exposure to salt water. Below the centerline another type of anti-fouling paint is applied; it also contains copper compounds that turn the original Red Oxide paint a Chalk-Green color after salt water exposure.

No painted hull numbers or names are paint applied after all publicity photos are taken; instead, at the discretion of the captain, magnetic hull numbers may be applied while in port. The only way that you can identify which sub is which, while in port, is to look at the baseball style caps that are worn by the enlisted personnel. The caps identify the hull number and name of the sub. The only other external color on a sub is the draft and projection (PROJ) marks painted in White on the hull. The projection marks are to warn tugs and docking crews that at the PROJ marking there is an external projection. The periscopes, snorkel and other extendable objects are painted in a Medium Gray with Dark Gray mottle to break up their outline while at sea.

The FBM submarine has long been the strongest arm of the U.S. Nuclear Triad policy. The Triad consists of separate and distinct forces designed to protect the United States from attack. The Triad is composed of the nuclear bomber forces and the land based strategic missile forces, both operated by the U.S. Air force and the FBM submarine forces. A fleet ballistic missile submarine operating in the vast expanses of the seven seas is almost undetectable and for over thirty years it has provided a secure nuclear deterrent force that has finally convinced the unfriendly elements around the world that it was time to come to terms with the peaceful people of the free world.

The following was sent to me by the crew of the USS ALASKA (SSBN 732):

The Submariner

Only a submariner realizes to what great extent an entire ship depends on him as an individual. To a land man this is not understandable and sometimes it is difficult for us to comprehend, but it is so!

A submarine at sea is a different world in herself, and in consideration of the protracted and distant operations of submarines, the Navy must place responsibility and trust in the hands of those who take such ships to sea.

In each submarine there men who, in hour of emergency or peril at sea, can turn to each other. These men are ultimately responsible to themselves and to each other for all aspects of operations of their submarine. They are the crew. They are the ship.

This is perhaps the most difficult and demanding assignment in the Navy. There is not an instance during his tour as a submariner that he can escape the grasp of responsibility. His privileges in view of his obligations are ludicrously small, never the less, it is the spur which has given the Navy its greatest mariners, the men of the submarine service.

It is a duty which most richly deserves the proud and time honored title of — SUBMARINER.

The missile tube compartment aboard the USS KENTUCKY. The tubes are painted in progressively lighter or darker shades of Orange depending on if you are looking forward or aft in the compartment. The Orange painted surfaces throughout the sub are designed to help the crew preserve their depth perception. (Al Adcock IV)

U.S. Warships
in action

4002

4004

4003

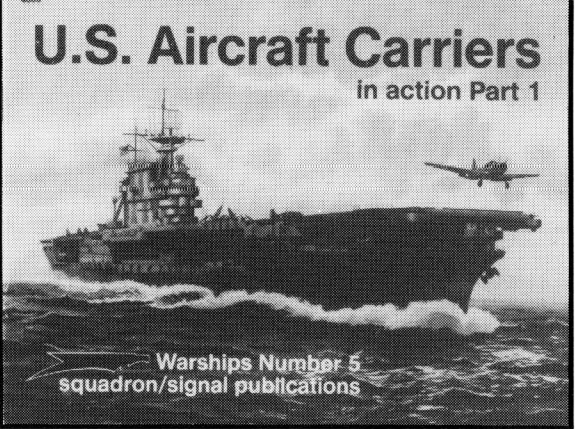
4005

squadron/signal publications